Portland Community College

WITHDRAWN

SCIENCE

FOUNDATIONS

Plate Tectonics

SCIENCE FOUNDATIONS

The Big Bang
Cell Theory
Electricity and Magnetism
The Expanding Universe
The Genetic Code
Germ Theory
Gravity
Heredity
Natural Selection
Planetary Motion
Plate Tectonics
Quantum Theory
Radioactivity
The Theory of Relativity

SCIENCE FOUNDATIONS

Plate Tectonics

STEPHEN M. TOMECEK

CHELSEA HOUSE
PUBLISHERS
An imprint of Infobase Publishing

To my professor Alan Ludman, a great geologist
who taught me how to "read the rocks."

Plate Tectonics

Copyright © 2009 by Infobase Publishing

Chelsea House
An imprint of Infobase Publishing
132 West 31st Street
New York NY 10001

Library of Congress Cataloging-in-Publication Data

Tomecek, Steve.
  Plate tectonics / Steve Tomecek.
     p. cm. — (Science foundations)
  Includes bibliographical references and index.
   ISBN 978-1-60413-014-0 (hardcover : acid-free paper) 1. Plate tectonics—Popular
works. I. Title. II. Series.
  QE511.4.T66 2009
  551.1'36—dc22   2008006054

Chelsea House books are available at special discounts when purchased in bulk quanti-
ties for businesses, associations, institutions, or sales promotions. Please call our Special
Sales Department in New York at (212) 967-8800 or (800) 322-8755.

You can find Chelsea House on the World Wide Web at
http://www.chelseahouse.com

Text design and composition by Kerry Casey
Cover design by Ben Peterson
Cover printed by Yurchak Printing, Landisville, Pa.
Book printed and bound by Yurchak Printing, Landisville, Pa.

Printed in the United States of America

This book is printed on acid-free paper.

All links and Web addresses were checked and verified to be correct at the time of publication. Because of the dynamic nature of the Web, some addresses and links may have
changed since publication and may no longer be valid.

Contents

1 Reading the Rocks   7

2 Drifting Continents   18

3 Radioactivity Heats Things Up   36

4 Under the Sea   49

5 Getting the Inside Story   64

6 Putting Plate Tectonic Theory   79
   to the Test

Glossary   89

Bibliography   94

Further Resources   95

Picture Credits   97

Index   98

About the Author   102

Reading the Rocks

Every so often, a new idea comes along in science that completely changes the way that people think about the world around them. These ideas are so radical that they are known as "scientific revolutions." For astronomers, one such revolution took place in the year 1543. Before this time, most people believed that Earth was the center of the universe and the Sun, stars, and planets all moved around us. Then an astronomer named Nicolaus Copernicus published a book suggesting that the Sun and stars stayed still and it was Earth that moved. It took over 100 years for this "Copernican revolution" to take hold. This idea completely changed the way that people viewed the solar system and our planet's place in it.

For biologists, a great revolution took place in 1859 when Charles Darwin published his book *On the Origin of Species by Means of Natural Selection*. In this book, Darwin presented his ideas about how different animals and plants evolved from other animals and plants. This "evolution revolution" gave biologists a whole new way of looking at living things and how they relate to each other.

For geologists, one of the most important scientific revolutions happened back in the mid-1960s. Unlike the work of Copernicus and Darwin, few people outside of the scientific community even noticed it happening. This revolution was the theory of plate tectonics. Plate tectonics describes how the outer surface of the Earth is made up of a number of large chunks called "plates." Because of forces inside the planet, these plates are in constant motion. As they move, they continuously change the size and the shape of the oceans and continents.

These days, plate tectonic theory is accepted by almost all geologists and is taught to science students from elementary school right up through college. In the early part of the twentieth century, however, the idea that Earth's crust could move was thought to be impossible. Those scientists who dared to suggest such an idea were attacked by other scientists who did not believe in these radical new ideas. Amazingly, in just a few short years, this revolutionary theory changed the way that scientists looked at our planet. It also provided the answers to many of the nagging questions that had haunted geologists for hundreds of years.

Unlike some other scientific revolutions, the theory of plate tectonics was not proposed by a single person—instead, it was the result of many different scientists all assembling different pieces to help solve a great puzzle. The development of plate tectonic theory is an excellent example of the scientific method in action, and its story reads more like a detective novel than a history book. To really appreciate just how revolutionary the theory of plate tectonics is, we must first take a step back in time and see how the science of geology got its start.

HOW GEOLOGISTS WORK

Geology is the science that studies both the makeup of and changes that happen to Earth. Unlike astronomy, physics, and biology, which can trace their origins back thousands of years, geology is a fairly young science that goes back only a few hundred years. As they develop their theories, geologists often draw information from other sciences such as physics, chemistry, and biology. Modern-day geologists use a great many high-tech tools to assist them in their work. In geology's early days, however, just about the only thing that scientists had to work with were rocks. To the untrained eye, rocks may not seem too exciting. In fact, even today,

What Makes a Scientific Theory?

To a scientist, the word *theory* means much more than a simple guess or idea. Before something can be considered a scientific theory, it has to go through many steps, a process known as the "scientific method." The scientific method begins with a series of observations that lead to a question about the way something works. Based on these observations, a scientist will then come up with one or more **hypotheses** to explain what is going on. Before a hypothesis can be considered a theory, scientists will design experiments to test the idea over and over again. During these tests, the hypothesis can be accepted, revised, or thrown out altogether.

Once they have finished their tests, scientists will report on the results of their experiments and get input from other scientists. Only after a hypothesis has stood up to all the experiments and testing, and after many scientists have accepted (or reached a *consensus*) that it is correct, can it be considered a scientific theory. As you will soon discover, the theory of plate tectonics has been tested over and over again, and even though it is relatively new, it has stood the test of time.

most people have a hard time telling one rock type from another. To a geologist, however, different rocks contain clues that help unlock the secrets of our planet's past. Questions about how Earth formed and how old it is can all be answered by "reading the rocks." Just like reading a book requires that you understand some basic rules about language, geologists follow some simple rules when they study rocks.

One of the first things that early geologists discovered was that not all rocks form the same way. One type of rock, called an **igneous rock**, forms from hot melted rock as it cools over time. Geologists call molten rock **magma**. Sometimes, as with a **volcano**, magma flows out over the surface of the Earth. When this happens,

Figure 1.1   The Hawaiian volcano Kilauea has been erupting continuously since 1983.

the molten rock is called **lava**. Every minute of every day, somewhere on Earth, lava erupts from volcanoes to eventually form new igneous rocks.

Not all rocks come from magma. Sometimes, small pieces of broken rock called **sediment** get squeezed or cemented together to form a new rock. Since they are made from sediment, these "recycled" rocks are called **sedimentary rocks**. Sedimentary rocks usually form in water when layers of sand, silt, and clay pile up on the bottom. Sedimentary rock can also form on land, but not as often as they form in water. Sometimes, sedimentary rocks will trap the remains of living things in them. Objects like shells, footprints, and bones that are preserved in sedimentary rocks are called **fossils**. Fossils found in sedimentary rocks provide geologists with important clues about how life on our planet has changed over time.

CATASTROPHISM MAKES A SPLASH

In the early part of the 1700s, most of the people who studied the Earth believed that our planet had changed very little over time. They believed that the rocks, mountains, and oceans that they saw had been created at the same time that Earth first formed. Earth itself was thought to be approximately 6,000 years old. However, this age was not based on the work of scientists—it was proposed by religious scholars who based their estimate on the story of Earth's creation as it was described in the Bible. (In fact, back in 1658, Archbishop James Ussher of Ireland calculated that the exact year of creation was 4004 B.C.)

As time went on, people who were looking for places to mine coal and iron realized that these valuable materials could be found

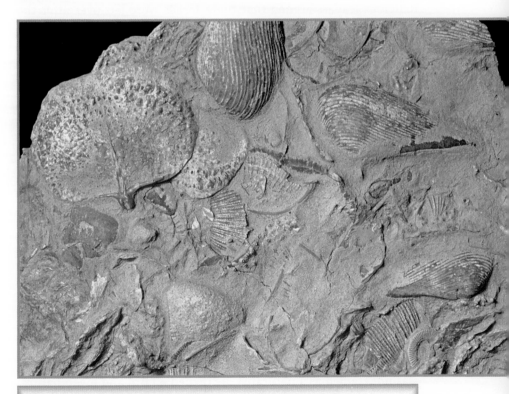

Figure 1.2 Some fossils may be found in limestone, a sedimentary rock.

near certain types of rocks. As a result, they turned to "naturalists" to make detailed maps of the local rocks. Naturalists were trained to make careful observations about the world around them, and the more they observed, the more they began to question some of the long-held ideas about Earth.

One of the first ideas that these trained observers began to question was the belief that Earth did not change over time. As they drew up their maps, naturalists often came across fossils of fish and other sea creatures high in the mountains, far from any ocean. The only logical conclusion was that these mountains must have been once covered with a great deal of water sometime in the past. How did the water get there? Where did it all go? It seemed some great changes had taken place.

Religious leaders offered an answer: The Bible tells a famous story about Noah and a great flood that covered the entire Earth. Religious leaders argued that these fossils were left over after the floodwaters went away. The Bible had stories about other catastrophes and many scientists believed that these events caused all of the changes that they saw in the rocks. This idea became known as **catastrophism**, and it gained a great deal of support. One of the biggest champions of this idea was Georges Cuvier, one of the most famous scientists of his day. There was a problem with this idea, though: Every time observations showed evidence of another change in the rocks, catastrophists would have to come up with another catastrophic event to explain it. As you might imagine, things got pretty messy in a hurry.

UNIFORMITARIANISM: SLOW AND STEADY WINS THE RACE

While catastrophists such as Cuvier attributed the characteristics of rocks to Biblical events, other scientists were looking for another answer to the problem. One of the most influential of them was a Scottish doctor named James Hutton. Even though Hutton was not trained as a naturalist, he owned a farm and loved nature. Much of his farm was covered with large rocks that he carefully studied. Over time, his observations stirred in him a real passion for geology.

In his studies of rocks, Hutton noticed certain patterns that seemed familiar. For example, in sedimentary rocks like sandstone and shale, he observed how each layer of sediment had been deposited on top of another layer of sediment below it. When he took a close look in areas where streams flowed into lakes, he discovered the exact same pattern of sedimentary layers. Hutton concluded that the sedimentary layers he saw in the rock had been created in the same way as the layers of sediment he saw in the lake. In fact, the process was exactly the same. Other naturalists had made the same observations, but Hutton took them one step further.

Hutton calculated how fast sedimentary layers were forming in the lake and realized that it would take years just to get a few inches of sediment to build up. He then began to look at the cliffs in the countryside around where he lived. Some of these cliffs were

James Hutton and John Playfair

While Hutton was a great scientist, it turns out that he was a terrible writer. Even though his books included numerous examples to support his theory, his writing style was so bad that few people could understand what he was trying to say. Fortunately, Hutton had a friend named John Playfair who was a professor of mathematics at Edinburgh University. Playfair was very familiar with Hutton's ideas because the two men frequently discussed them. After Hutton died, Playfair was afraid that his friend's work would be forgotten. Even though he was not a geologist, Playfair understood Hutton's theory well enough to write about it. Unlike Hutton, Playfair was a gifted writer, and in 1802, he published a book titled *Illustrations of the Huttonian Theory of the Earth*. In this book, Playfair clearly outlined the concept of uniformitarianism. The tide slowly turned as other scientists read Playfair's book and began to accept the idea. The real breakthrough came in the early 1800s when a young geologist named Charles Lyell picked up on the idea and became its new champion.

made of sedimentary rocks that had layers that were hundreds of feet thick. To get this much sediment built up would take a lot of time—not just hundreds or thousands, but *millions* of years. To Hutton, there was only one answer—Earth had to be much older than 6,000 years.

After making many more detailed observations, Hutton was convinced that he was correct. In 1785, he wrote down his ideas in two papers that were presented to the Royal Society in Edinburgh, Scotland. His central idea was a simple one. Instead of Earth's changes being caused by large, catastrophic events in the past, Hutton proposed that all of the geologic features we see in ancient rocks can be explained by processes that can be observed in action today. "The present is the key to the past" is the saying most often used by geologists to express this idea. These small, steady *uniform* changes acting over a long period of time were all that were needed to make the large changes that took place in the Earth. This idea became known as the principle of **uniformitarianism**, one of the most important concepts used in geology today.

As you might expect, when Hutton's papers were finally published in 1788, many of the leading scientists of the time thought he was totally wrong. But while he was strongly criticized and mocked, he refused to back down. In 1795, he published his findings in a two-volume book titled *Theory of the Earth,* in which he provided dozens of examples to support his ideas. In his discussion of the age of the Earth, he said, "We find no vestige of a beginning—no prospect of an end." In other words, he was suggesting that the age of the Earth was too old even to calculate. This was a major change from what was accepted as truth at the time.

Hutton took a big risk in publishing his book because not only did he go against what most scientists believed, but he was also seen as challenging religious beliefs, too. He would have had to face a great deal of public criticism, but he died in March 1797 before these forces could gather steam.

Sir Charles Lyell's New Ideas About Very Old Rocks

Charles Lyell was born in Scotland in November 1797, eight months after James Hutton had died. The Lyell family was fairly well off. Charles Senior, Lyell's father, was a lawyer. As young Charles grew up, it was planned that he become a lawyer, too, but he had other ideas.

In 1816, Lyell entered Exeter College, where he showed a real talent for math and science. He became interested in geology after reading Playfair's book and was fascinated with the idea of uniformitarianism.

During the summer of 1817, Lyell attended several lectures given at Oxford University by William Buckland, a geologist who also was a big supporter of Hutton's theory. After Buckland showed Lyell some new, detailed geological maps of England, Lyell decided that geology was going to become his profession. This did not sit well with his father, so Lyell continued to study law while keeping his work in geology in the background. Over the course of the next few years, Charles took many trips around England and Europe and made careful observations of the rocks wherever he went. He completed his law degree in 1822 and began working as a lawyer while continuing to study geology on the side. He joined the newly formed Geological Society of London and became their secretary.

In 1825, Lyell was asked to write an article for the *Quarterly Review,* a journal that published essays about many topics, including the latest developments in science. Like John Playfair, he was a talented writer and was paid well for his work. By 1827, Lyell gave up his law practice to become a full-time author. He decided his first book would be about geology. Rather than redo what others had done, Lyell wanted to see for himself how different geological principles worked. He set off on a year-long expedition to Europe where he met with local geologists and took extensive field notes. When he returned to London in February 1829, he began work on the book. In July 1830, the first volume of his *Principles of Geology* was published. It became a big hit.

Lyell's *Principles* clearly laid out the most up-to-date theories about Earth and gave detailed descriptions of how slow, steady forces acting over time shaped the planet. His examples were so clear that, even though he didn't have a degree in science, he was offered the position of Chair of Geology at King's College in London. In this new position, Lyell gave numerous public lectures on geology. (He

The New Catastrophists

These days, most geologists accept the principle of uniformatarianism and use it in their work. Most of them also believe that, from time to time, large catastrophes have also occurred—giant earthquakes, tsunamis, volcanic eruptions, and even impacts from extraterrestrial objects, such as asteroids and comets, have all had an impact on Earth. These types of catastrophic events still happen today. However, geologists classify these events as following the general rule of uniformitarianism rather catastrophism. Whereas events such as asteroid impacts cause understandable and predictable effects that follow physical laws, events such as a biblical flood would have been a one-time-only event that left no evidence that it actually occurred. The difference between modern-day catastrophists and those of the past is that even those geologists who acknowledge the Earth-shaping power of catastrophies believe that most of the changes that we see acting on Earth are thought to be due to slow, steady processes acting over time.

Figure 1.3   Meteor Crater in Arizona is one of the best known meteorite craters in the world—and a good example of the results of a catastrophe.

even encouraged women to attend the lectures, which was unheard of at the time.) When he was not lecturing, he was writing, revising his original book and publishing two more volumes of his *Principles.* In 1833, he resigned from King's College to concentrate on his research and writing.

Over the next 40 years, Lyell, accompanied by his wife, Mary Lyell, continued to do field work and update his books. In 1838, he published *Elements of Geology*, which was the first modern textbook on geology. In 1841, he was knighted.

Even though Hutton was the first one to explain the ideas behind uniformitarianism, it was Lyell's work that finally put to rest the idea of catastrophism and caused scientists to accept the idea that small changes acting over a long time could bring about large changes in the Earth. In his second volume of the *Principles,* Lyell offered an idea about how different animals and plant species changed over time. Based on his observations of fossils, he concluded that many more species must have lived on Earth in the past. These living things went extinct but were replaced by new species. This idea formed the backbone of Charles Darwin's work on evolution almost 25 years later. Darwin himself gave credit to Lyell for setting the stage for his theory of evolution, but he was not the only scientist to be so influenced. In the early 1900s, a German scientist named Alfred Wegener would use the principle of uniformitarianism to put forth his own theory of how the position of the continents themselves had changed over time. His radical idea would be the first piece placed in the plate tectonic puzzle.

2

Drifting Continents

The first step in the development of modern plate tectonic theory can be traced back to the early days of the twentieth century and an idea that became known as **continental drift**. Simply stated, continental drift is the hypothesis that all of the landmasses on Earth were joined together into one giant "supercontinent" at some time in the distant past. Over millions of years, this single landmass slowly broke apart and the continents gradually "drifted" into the positions that we see them in today.

As you might expect, when this idea was first proposed, most scientists were dead set against it. After all, the idea that the continents had somehow moved over time was directly opposed to the idea that Earth was a solid, stable planet. Was there any evidence to suggest that such a radical concept may have been possible? Yes—all that is needed is a map of the world.

By looking at a map of the world, even a nonscientist can see a very striking pattern. For example, in the southern Atlantic Ocean, the east coast of South America and the west coast of Africa appear to be near-perfect matches for each other. Moving up to the North Atlantic, the coasts of Europe and North America also seem to fit. Moving Greenland south a bit would slide it into a wedge-shaped space there. It is almost like these continents were pieces in some global jigsaw puzzle.

The truth is, long before the idea of continental drift was proposed, some people had noted these similarities and were raising

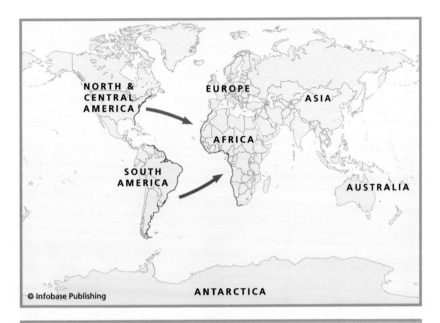

Figure 2.1 By examining a map of the world, one can see how the coasts of North America and South America seem to fit together with the coasts of Europe and Africa, as if the continents were once part of a big jigsaw puzzle.

questions about them. Soon after Columbus made his historic voyages back in the late 1400s, mapmakers began drawing what they thought the Atlantic Ocean looked like. As more details became available and the maps got better, people started to wonder if the continents might have once been connected together.

In his work *Thesaurus Geographicus,* published in 1596, the Dutch mapmaker Abraham Ortelius suggested that Europe and Africa might have been torn apart by "earthquakes and floods." Later, in 1666, a French naturalist named Francois Paget suggested that the reason the coastlines looked as if they fit together was due to the sinking of a large section of land down into the Earth, after which the seas rushed into the gap to form the Atlantic Ocean.

For most geologists working in the seventeenth and eighteenth centuries, however, the shape of the continents was thought to be

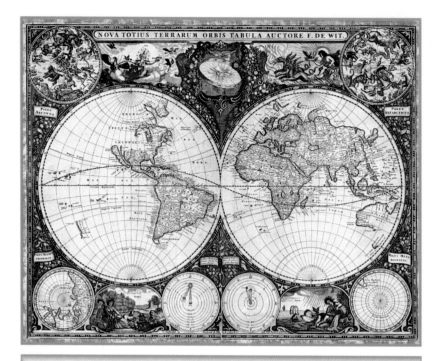

Figure 2.2 This antique map of the world shows how scientists of the eighteenth century thought the continents were configured. Not all parts of the world had been extensively mapped by Europeans yet, which is represented by blank spaces such as the one covering what we now know to be the northwest corner of North America.

a simple coincidence rather than something that needed further investigation. Once the ideas of Hutton and Lyell on uniformitarianism gained acceptance, though, a growing number of scientists became interested in the question again. As you might suspect, some of their theories seem pretty far fetched by today's standards.

EVIDENCE FOR A CONTRACTING EARTH

By the late 1800s, many scientists had started explaining the origins of Earth's surface features by using the principles of uniformitarianism. While many had no problem accepting the idea of small changes, a large number of geologists still thought that large-scale geologic features, like oceans, continents, and mountain chains, could only be formed by large catastrophic events.

One of the geologists working on the problem was an American named James Dana. Dana was a professor at Yale University and one of the most highly regarded scientists during the late 1800s. Like many geologists of his day, Dana believed that Earth had formed from a large molten ball that had been slowly cooling over time. He also believed that the inside of the planet was still filled with hot magma which produced volcanoes, but the magma that had flowed out onto the surface to become lava had cooled enough to make a solid rock crust.

Based on the work of other scientists, Dana knew that when matter cooled, it also contracted, or shrank in size. Using this information, Dana proposed the idea that, over time, Earth must have become smaller as it cooled. During this contraction, large wrinkles formed on its surface and caused large cracks. These cracks in turn gave the continents their present-day shapes and also produced all of the large mountain chains found on the planet.

At about the same time in Europe, another group of geologists were also looking at this idea of a contracting Earth to explain the shape of the continents. In Austria, a geologist named Eduard Suess came up with a theory that was similar to Dana's but did not follow the principles of uniformitarianism.

Like Dana, Suess also believed that Earth had cooled over time and was slowly contracting. He believed that the oceans were created when large chunks of the crust sank down into planet. The continents were simply those leftover pieces that remained on top. In addition, Suess believed that this sinking action happened in several sudden catastrophic jolts and were not the result of a slow, steady motion.

As it turned out, the theories of both Suess and Dana were wrong for one simple reason: Earth is not contracting. In fact, as far as we can tell, it has stayed pretty much the same size since it first formed. The important point about these early theories is that they showed that scientists were beginning to realize that the entire surface of Earth was not static, but had changed over time.

Figure 2.3 The Krafla area in Iceland, which still shows some volcanic activity, has cracks that run through it. James Dana and other geologists in the late 1800s thought cracks like this were proof that the Earth was contracting, but we now know that features like this are caused by the slow shifting of tectonic plates.

Eduard Suess Names Gondwanaland

Eduard Suess was born in London in 1831. As a youngster, he and his family moved to Austria. After completing his degree in geology, he went to work at the Hofmuseum in Vienna, where he spent much of his time studying and classifying the fossils of ancient sea creatures. In 1857, he wrote a small book on the origin of the Alps, and in the same year he began working as a professor of geology at the University of Vienna.

Over the next 40 years, Suess worked on his theory of the contracting Earth. Even though his ideas would later be proven wrong, he gave the world an important name: *Gondwana*. According to Suess, Gondwana was a giant landmass that had existed in the Southern Hemisphere and included India, Africa, Australia, South America, and Antarctica. While his ideas about how these continents formed were wrong, the name Gondwana has stuck. It is used by geologists today to describe a giant "supercontinent" that broke apart to form these smaller continents and is a major part of modern plate tectonic theory.

EARLY IDEAS ABOUT SHIFTING CONTINENTS

By the mid-1800s, geologists had collected a great deal of information about the rocks found along the coasts of North America, South America, Europe, and Africa. At this time, an American named Antonio Snider-Pellegrini was working in Paris where he had access to many of these geological reports. As he reviewed the data, Snider-Pellegrini noticed something interesting. Not only did the coastlines between the continents appear to match in shape, but so did many of the rock types found on each continent. It

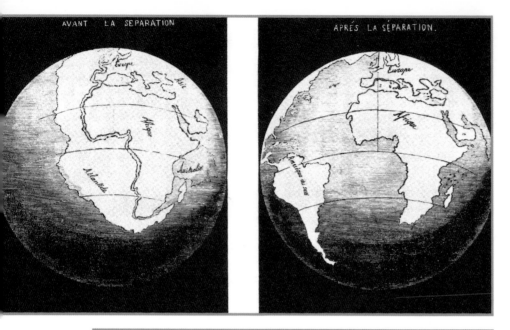

Figure 2.4 Antonio Snider-Pellegrini's maps show the American and African continents as separate and as one landmass, to illustrate that they fit together and were once connected. The map on the left shows how they fit together before their separation. His map on the right shows them after the separation.

seemed that fossils and coal deposits found on the continent on one side of the Atlantic Ocean also appeared on the continent on the opposite side.

Snider-Pellegrini became convinced that the Atlantic Ocean had formed as the result of some type of catastrophic event. This event, he believed, was also responsible for the great flood that was described in the Bible. He believed that during this event, a single landmass was torn apart followed by the movement of the continents into their present positions. He published his ideas in 1858 along with a map of the world with all of the continents assembled into one large landmass. Because his explanation of how the continents moved seemed impossible, few people took his idea seriously. His map, on the other hand, got a great deal of attention. Not only did the continents physically fit together, but so did many of the types of rocks each of them contained. To some scientists, the idea that the continents had once been assembled together seemed to be way more than a coincidence.

In 1908, another American named Frank Bursley Taylor picked up on some of Snider-Pellegrini's ideas and used them to explain where mountains came from. Taylor was an amateur geologist who was not connected to a famous university, so he was not considered to be an "expert" in his field. Taylor disagreed with the ideas presented by Dana and Suess that mountains formed when Earth had contracted. Using a map similar to the one drawn by Snider-Pellegrini, he showed that most major mountain belts appeared where continents had once been joined together. Mountains were caused, he suggested, not by wrinkles formed by the shrinking of Earth's crust, but by two continents sliding into each other, pushing the land at the point of contact upward. As it turned out, this idea would fit in well with modern plate tectonic theory. Unfortunately for Taylor, he came up with it about 60 years too soon: The few people who read about it at the time did not take it seriously.

ALFRED WEGENER TAKES ON THE WORLD

The scientific community quickly rejected Taylor's theory on mountain building. The idea of continents being able to move through a solid Earth seemed so far fetched that few serious geologists would accept it. That did not stop everyone from thinking about the idea, however. In the early 1900s, a German scientist named Alfred Wegener picked up on the concept and, before he was through, made many geologists think that the impossible might be possible.

Wegener was born in Berlin on November 1, 1880. While his childhood was uneventful, he did receive a strong background in science while attending the universities of Heidelberg, Innsbruck, and Berlin. Wegener was interested in many areas of natural science. He received his doctorate degree in astronomy in 1905, but was more interested in the new science of **meteorology** than in studying space. He began working for the Prussian Aeronautical

Observatory, where he experimented with using kites and balloons to take high-altitude weather readings.

Wegener was quickly making a name for himself as a meteorologist when, in 1906, he was invited to join a Danish expedition to study the climate of Greenland. For almost two years, he took detailed atmospheric readings of Greenland's severe weather patterns and perfected the use of tethered balloons. In 1908, he returned to Germany where he was offered a position at the University of Marburg, where he lectured on meteorology and astronomy. Wegener had a special ability to explain difficult topics in simple terms. He also stressed the importance of using data from other areas of science to help show how a topic fit into the "bigger picture."

While Wegener was working at Marburg, he became interested in the idea of continental drift. It is not known if he actually read the work of either Taylor or Snider-Pellegrini, but like the other scientists before him, he was fascinated with how the continents across the Atlantic Ocean seemed to fit together. In 1911, after reading a report about the similarity of fossils found in both Brazil and Africa, he became convinced that the continents had split apart long ago and "drifted" into their present positions. Wegener searched the literature for other geological reports and began collecting data supporting the idea. In January 1912, he presented his hypothesis at a meeting of the Geological Association in Frankfurt. The members of the group did not quite know what to make of this "weatherman" who was lecturing them on the topic of rocks.

Before he could pursue the theory further, Wegener joined another expedition to Greenland. While conducting his experiments, he faced many challenges, often spending days at a time camped out on the frozen ice. On more than on occasion, he cheated death. Once, he narrowly missed getting killed by falling ice when a glacier he was climbing on started to break up.

By the time he returned to Germany in 1913, Wegener was looked upon as a world authority on polar climates and glaciers. Just as he returned to work on his continental drift theory, however, World War I broke out. Wegener was drafted into the German army, where he served as a lieutenant and was wounded in

Figure 2.5 Alfred Wegener (1880-1930) filled in many gaps in the early continental drift theory, leading the way to the currently accepted theory of plate tectonics.

battle twice. While recovering in the hospital from his second wound, he finally had the time to write up his theory. In 1915, he published the first draft of his book, entitled *Die Entstehung der*

Alfred Wegener's Interdisciplinary Approach

Unlike Taylor, Dana, and Suess, Wegener presented an enormous amount of data from other areas of science to support his theory. In the final edition of *The Origins of Continents and Oceans,* Wegener wrote the following: "Scientists still do not appear to understand sufficiently that all Earth sciences must contribute evidence toward unveiling the state of our planet in earlier times, and the truth of the matter can only be reached by combining all this evidence." This idea became known as the "interdisciplinary approach" and was very different from the way that most scientists went about their business. When it came to the Earth sciences, most scientists just worked in their own fields. Mineralogists studied minerals, paleontologists studied fossils, and meteorologists were just supposed to study weather.

Wegener was different. He had a gift for seeing the "big picture" and was not afraid to work outside his field of expertise. Perhaps the fact that he was trained as an astronomer but spent most of his professional career working as a meteorologist gave him the confidence to "cross over" and use data from other scientific disciplines. As you might expect, the fact that he was a "weatherman doing geology" caused him a great many problems. Because his research and ideas were sound, however, he never backed down from other scientists who attacked his credentials. Today, his interdisciplinary approach is considered an acceptable way for a scientist to operate.

Kontinente und Ozeane, which translates in English to *The Origins of Continents and Oceans.*

The first draft of the book was only 94 pages long. This, plus the fact that war was still raging in Europe, meant that few took notice of Wegener's ideas. After leaving the hospital, he returned to active duty, working for the army's meteorological service. When World

War I finally ended in 1918, Wegener went to work at the German Marine Laboratory in Hamburg. There, he collected additional data to support his theory. He published revised editions of his book in both 1920 and 1922. The last edition was translated into several languages, including English, French, Spanish, and Russian. Once scientists outside Germany had the opportunity to read his ideas, things became very interesting indeed.

Wegener's Evidence for Continental Drift

Wegener began his argument for continental drift with some simple physics. He wanted to prove that it would be impossible for continental landmasses simply to sink into the Earth to produce the oceans.

Suess and others used the idea of a cooling, contracting Earth to explain how "land bridges" sank into the inner part of the planet to form the oceans. Using geological maps, Wegener showed that most of the rocks that made up the continents were made of **granite**, while those that made up the ocean floor were made of **basalt**. Granites are much less dense than basalts. Density is a property of matter that helps to control how things float. Objects with a low density naturally float, while objects with a high density naturally sink. Wegener argued that it would have been impossible for the less-dense continental rocks to sink through the much denser rocks under the oceans. To back this up, he used observations that he had made in Greenland. For example, he pointed out, icebergs float on the ocean because solid ice is less dense than liquid water. He suggested that the continents are really just "floating" on the denser rocks found underneath them.

This idea of rocks moving up and down due to differences in density was not new. Starting in the mid-nineteenth century, geologists had begun to use the idea of **isostasy**. This principle explains how the outer surface of the Earth can move up and down due to loading and unloading of material on top of it. Data from northern Europe and North America showed that during the last ice age, the weight of glaciers had pushed the land surface down into the Earth like a finger poking into a balloon. After the glaciers melted away, the weight was lifted and the ground surface began to "rebound." Wegener argued that if sections of Earth's surface could move up

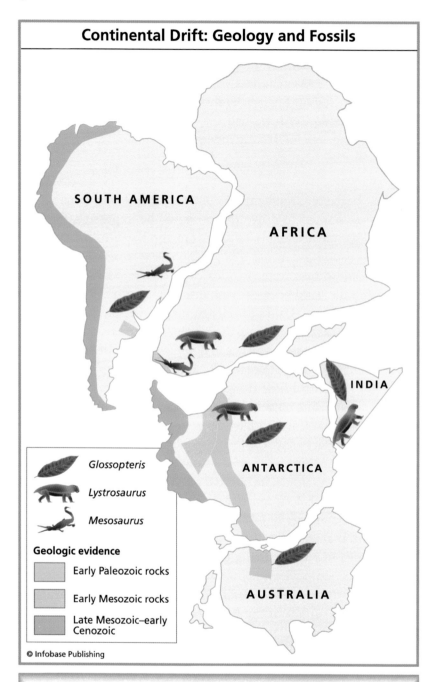

Continental Drift: Geology and Fossils

SOUTH AMERICA

AFRICA

INDIA

ANTARCTICA

AUSTRALIA

Glossopteris

Lystrosaurus

Mesosaurus

Geologic evidence

Early Paleozoic rocks

Early Mesozoic rocks

Late Mesozoic–early Cenozoic

© Infobase Publishing

Figure 2.6 The idea of continental drift is supported by the continuation of land forms, fossils, and rocks across continental boundaries.

and down, then they should also be able to move from side to side, too.

Once he explained how the continents could drift sideways, Wegener's next step was to offer evidence to show that they had once been joined together. Like Taylor before him, Wegener began his theory with a map of the world that showed how the continents

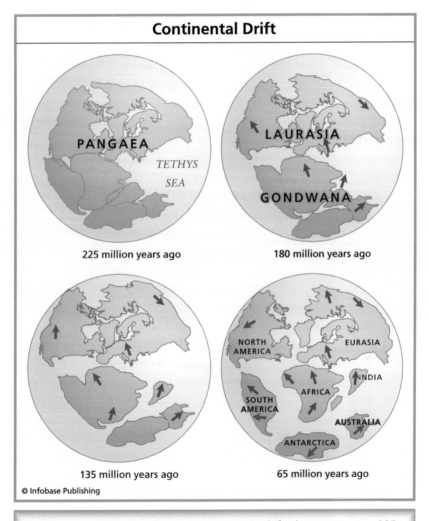

Figure 2.7   As time went on, the continents drifted apart, starting 225 million years ago when the supercontinent Pangaea (the name given by Alfred Wegener) broke up into continents.

could be fit back together again to make one large landmass. He called this single continent **Pangaea**, a word from the Greek language that means "all lands."

Next, Wegener outlined all the different types of data that he had assembled to prove that the continents had once been joined together. He started by showing how some mountain ranges would seem to cross over continental boundaries and continue on the other side. One such connection was between the Appalachian Mountains of North America and the Highlands in Scotland. He also showed that, in many cases, distinctive rock types and fossils found on one continent exactly matched those found on the opposite continent. To emphasize these connections, Wegener offered the following example: "It is just as if we were to refit the torn pieces of a newspaper by matching their edges and then check whether the lines of print ran smoothly across. If they do, there is nothing left but to conclude that the pieces were in fact joined in this way."

Some of Wegener's best evidence for the drifting of continents came from his work on climates. In many cases, he found situations where fossils and rock types did not match the climate of the present-day continents. For example, many fossils found on the island of Spitsbergen, located in the Arctic Ocean, were of animals and plants that could only have lived in a tropical environment. If Spitsbergen had not "drifted" into its present position, then how could it have had a tropical climate in the past? Another example came from the Sahara Desert, where there are sedimentary deposits called "tillites." These distinctive features are deposited by moving glaciers, the same type that Wegener studied in Greenland. Even the most skeptical geologist would have a hard time explaining how glacial deposits wound up in a desert located in the tropics.

After he presented all of the evidence supporting the idea that the continents had been joined in the past, Wegener offered the following conclusions: About 200 million years ago, the supercontinent Pangaea began to break up into smaller continents. As the continents began to drift apart, the Atlantic and Indian oceans started to form. Mountain ranges like the Himalayas and the Alps formed as a result of one continent crashing into another and causing their rocks to be pushed up into mountain ranges.

Unfortunately, despite all his excellent evidence, the one thing Wegener didn't offer was a good explanation for how and why the continents moved. This would open the door for his many critics, who were just waiting to attack the "weatherman" who dared to do geology.

Wegener Faces His Critics

To say that Wegener's theory was not entirely accepted would be a gross understatement. After the different translations of the third edition of his book came out in 1922, scientists all over the world lined up to take shots at him. In many cases, the simple fact that he was not a geologist was enough to set people against him. Many scientists felt that a man who had no real training in geology had no business writing about the subject. Some of them simply refused even to read his work. They were incensed that this "weatherman" would dare to lecture them on something as critical as the origins of the continents and oceans.

Many of those who read the theory were troubled by his explanation of how the continents moved. Basically, what Wegener suggested was that the solid continents moved through the solid ocean crust without disturbing it in any way. This would be like a boat moving through water without leaving any wake behind it. Based on the evidence, this did not appear to be the case. Another problem was that Wegener conveniently left out the data that did not appear to support a match between continents. This raised the suspicions of many scientists who wondered what else he may have left out of his book.

Another problem that hurt Wegener's theory was the fact that some of his data were flat out wrong. For example, he predicted that the Atlantic Ocean was growing by over 98.4 inches (250 cm) per year and that Greenland had broken away from the rest of Scandinavia less than 100,000 years ago. These numbers were looked at as being impossibly high because they were just that.

Perhaps the biggest problem was Wegener's explanation for the forces that caused the continents to move. The best idea that he could come up with involved a combination of tides and centrifugal force created by the spin of the Earth. To geologists (and the rest of the scientific community), this did not make any sense. Neither of these forces was strong enough to move anything as big and massive as a continent. Wegener knew it was a problem and he tried to hedge. In the final edition of his book, he wrote: "It is probable that the complete solution of the problem of the forces will be a long time coming." About this issue, he was correct!

Despite his critics, Wegener passionately defended his theory. He tried to get a professorship at a university in Germany so that he could continue his research. He was repeatedly turned down for the job, in part because of all the controversy he had caused. Finally, in 1924, the University of Graz in Austria offered him a position to teach meteorology. Even though his continental drift theory was unpopular, his reputation as a meteorologist was still outstanding. While at Graz, Wegener continued to gather evidence for his theory and, in 1929, published the fourth and final edition of his book. In it, he tried to answer many of his critics. Sadly, it would be the last time he would be able to defend his theory for himself.

Alfred Wegener's Untimely Death

In the spring of 1930, Wegener launched another expedition to Greenland, in part to get better data on how fast the island was drifting. When he arrived in Greenland, he found that weather conditions were terrible. Extreme cold and frequent storms caused many delays. Several team members had set up an inland weather station that was in desperate need of supplies. Rather than having someone else do the job, Wegener led the supply team himself. For five weeks, they trekked across the frozen ice, enduring temperatures that reached 54 degrees below zero (-48° C).

Wegener finally reached the camp with the supplies, but rather than spending a few days to rest, he decided to return to the base camp on the coast to resume his research. Wegener left with his guide on November 1, 1930, which happened to be his 50th birthday. It was the last time the two men were ever seen alive. On May 12, 1931, a search team found Wegener's body wrapped in his sleeping bag, buried in the snow in between two skis that were standing straight up. Rather than remove the body, the team built an ice structure around it as a monument to the polar explorer and father of the theory of continental drift.

While it is unfortunate that Wegener never lived to see his ideas accepted, he probably would have been pleased with the final outcome. As it turned out, not every scientist dismissed his ideas. Even before he died, new discoveries in science were unlocking other pieces of the puzzle. Even though the idea of continental drift initially left way too many unanswered questions, without Wegener's work, the theory of plate tectonics might never have become a reality.

3

Radioactivity Heats Things Up

After Alfred Wegener's death in 1930, much of the controversy over continental drift began to die down. Most scientists felt that there were just too many flaws in the theory to give it much serious consideration. Rather than pursue it further, they went about their business conducting research in other areas of geology. Nevertheless, Wegener's ideas did not completely die out.

In South Africa, a geologist named Alexander Du Toit firmly believed that Wegener's reconstruction of Pangaea was correct. He continued working on the problem after Wegener's death and produced even more evidence to show that connections between the continents had existed in the past. In Switzerland, another geologist named Emile Argand was convinced that continental drift was the best way to explain the formation of mountains like the Alps. Argand's field work led him to conclude that the huge folds of rocks found in the mountains could only be produced by continents smashing together.

Unfortunately, the biggest question about the theory still went unanswered: What type of force could actually move something the size of a continent through the Earth? The answer would be found thanks to a newly discovered energy source called **radioactivity**. Not only would radioactivity provide the means for making conti-

Figure 3.1   The folded strata, or rock layers, are visible in the horizontal bands along this cliff face in Austria. The folds provide evidence of tectonic forces pushing against each other in the Earth's crust.

nents move, but it would also provide an "atomic clock" that would finally allow scientists to determine an age for Earth.

Back in 1896, a French physicist named Henri Becquerel made an astonishing discovery. He was conducting studies on a newly discovered form of energy called the X-ray and trying to find out whether these mysterious rays were produced by any natural materials. He had stored a container filled with salts of the element uranium in a desk drawer along with some new photographic plates. When he retrieved the plates, he found that they had somehow been exposed. When he developed the plates, he found they contained images of the uranium salt crystals—some invisible energy source from the salt crystals was causing changes in the plates. Two years later, Marie and Pierre Curie came up with a name for this mysterious phenomena: radioactivity. The energy that came from these special materials was called **radiation**.

During their research, the Curies discovered that many naturally occurring minerals typically found in the Earth are radioactive. When these minerals release their radiation, they also release heat. (It is this heat from radioactive elements that engineers use in modern-day nuclear power plants to make steam to generate electricity.)

Picking up where the Curies left off, an English physicist named Ernest Rutherford made another amazing discovery. Scientists had long believed that atoms were the smallest particle that matter could be divided into. They also believed that atoms themselves could not change. An atom of oxygen would always stay an atom of oxygen, and an atom of carbon would always be carbon. Rutherford found that this was not always the case. Atoms of radioactive elements did change: Over time, uranium atoms would turn into atoms of lead, a process that took place in a very predictable way.

RELATIVE VS. ABSOLUTE TIME

One of the biggest problems that geologists have when trying to piece together the history of our planet is figuring out how old different rocks are. Before the twentieth century, the best that they could do was to come up with a **relative age date**. A relative age date can help estimate which rock is older when it is compared with another, but it does not tell *how old* the rock actually is.

What Causes Radioactivity?

To understand how radioactivity can change one type of atom into another, we must first look at what an atom is made of. Atoms have two main parts. First, in the center of the atom, is the nucleus. This is where most of the mass of an atom is located. The nucleus is made up of two different particles: protons, which have a positive charge, and neutrons, which have no charge. The second main part contains even smaller particles that move around the outside of the nucleus: These particles are called electrons. Electrons have a negative charge, and they produce electricity.

Each type of element has its own special atom with a different number of protons in the nucleus. For example, an oxygen atom has eight protons in its nucleus, while a helium nucleus has only two protons. Scientists have discovered over 100 different elements, each with a different number of protons in the nucleus. As it turns out, many of the elements that have the largest atoms are radioactive. For example, the most common form of the element uranium is called U-238. It has 92 protons and 146 neutrons in its nucleus. All of these particles jammed together in such a small space means that the uranium nucleus is very unstable.

Every so often, some of the protons and neutrons break up and the nucleus will eject the particles as different types of radiation. When this happens, scientists say that the element undergoes **radioactive decay**. This happens when a neutron of an atom changes to become a proton. As a result, the atom changes into the atom of a different element. A neutron of an atom can also change to become a proton. These types of changes are called *beta decay*.

Most radioactive elements actually decay several times, changing in a step-like fashion until they finally turn into an atom that is stable. This is called a decay series and it happens in a very predictable manner.

Using the principles described by Charles Lyell and several other geologists, scientists working in the eighteenth and nineteenth centuries did some remarkable work. By using fossils to link up

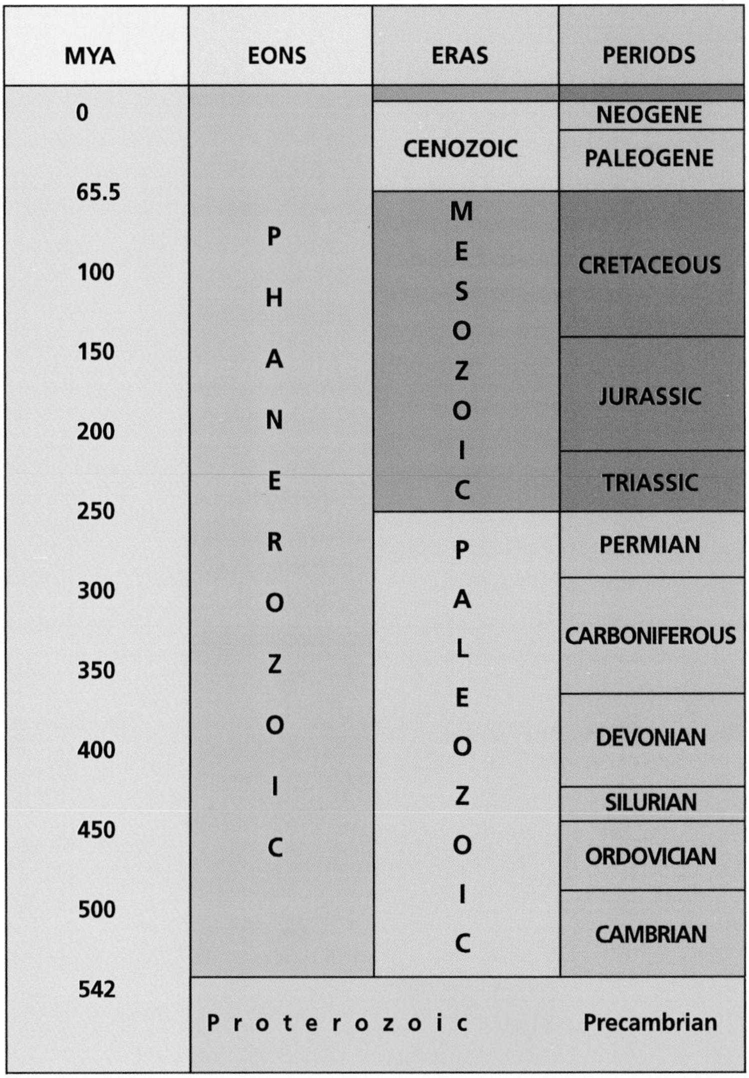

MYA	EONS	ERAS	PERIODS
0		CENOZOIC	NEOGENE
			PALEOGENE
65.5		M E S O Z O I C	
100	P H A N E R O Z O I C		CRETACEOUS
150			JURASSIC
200			
250			TRIASSIC
		P A L E O Z O I C	PERMIAN
300			CARBONIFEROUS
350			
400			DEVONIAN
			SILURIAN
450			ORDOVICIAN
500			CAMBRIAN
542	Proterozoic		Precambrian

Figure 3.2 Scientists created a geologic time scale by studying rock layers to divide the Earth's history into different time periods.

rock layers from different areas of the planet, they slowly built up a *geologic time scale* for the planet. This chart neatly divided Earth history into different time segments called eons, eras, periods, and epochs.

Having a relative time scale to work with was very helpful, but what geologists really needed was a way of telling **absolute time**. An absolute age date tells you how old something is in terms of years. With an absolute time scale, geologists could tell exactly how old Earth was. It would also allow them to calculate how fast different changes took place.

By the end of the 1800s, several scientists had used some rather ingenious ways to try and calculate the absolute age of Earth. For example, in 1897, British physicist William Thomson (who would later be known as Lord Kelvin) used the cooling of Earth to come up with an age of about 40 million years for the planet. He got this number by calculating how long it would take for Earth to reach its current temperature if it started in a completely molten state. In 1899, another British scientist named John Joly came up with an age of about 90 million years. He based this figure on the concentration of salt in the ocean. By measuring the average salt content of streams, Joly estimated how long it would take to build up the current amount of salt in seawater. Neither of these estimates was even close to the correct number. This would change, though, when an American scientist named Bertram Boltwood used radioactive decay to finally get an accurate age for Earth.

BERTRAM BOLTWOOD INVENTS "ATOMIC TIME"

Once Ernest Rutherford discovered the basics of how radioactive decay worked, scientists suddenly had a new tool at their disposal. Bertram Borden Boltwood was born in Amherst, Massachusetts, in 1870. At the age of 19, he entered Yale University and graduated with honors in only 3 years with a degree in chemistry. Boltwood spent the next two years in Germany at the University of Munich where he studied rare earth minerals, including many that contained the element uranium. Returning to Yale, he received his doctorate degree in chemistry in 1897.

After graduation, Boltwood teamed up with a classmate to run his own lab, and it was at this time that he first learned about the discoveries of Becquerel and the Curies. It was after reading several papers on radioactivity written by Ernest Rutherford that Boltwood began his own research into this new form of energy. He quickly became recognized as one of the leading authorities on radioactivity in the United States. In the process, he also became friends with Ernest Rutherford, with whom he frequently corresponded. Rutherford thought that it should be possible to calculate how old a rock was by measuring the amount of radioactive decay taking place in it. Boltwood was intrigued by the idea and began working on the problem.

In studying the radioactive decay of the element uranium, Boltwood found that the stable end product was always a form of the element lead. He figured that if a rock contained uranium, then the older it was, the more lead should be present. By comparing the amount of lead to the amount of uranium in the sample, he should be able to calculate the age of the rock. All he would need to know is the rate at which the uranium turned to lead. This number—called the **half-life**—would be something he could measure in the lab.

In 1907, Boltwood began to work with several different rock samples in his lab. His calculations astounded him: One sample was dated at over 500 million years old, while a second one came in at over 2 billion years. While the work of Hutton and Lyell led many geologists to conclude that Earth had to be old, these numbers were older than anyone had ever imagined up to that time.

Boltwood continued to work on his measurements and refined the age dating process. His later tests showed that the results were accurate. Earth was not a few hundred million years old—it was *billions* of years old. Boltwood had given geologists the exact tool they were looking for—an accurate geologic clock that was built right into the rocks! Using Boltwood's techniques, geologists have determined that our Earth is about 4.6 billion years old. Given this much time, it's easy to see how the slow steady changes that were proposed by Hutton and Lyell could easily reshape the entire planet.

How Does
Radioactive Age Dating Work?

The idea behind radioactive age dating is really quite simple. When igneous rocks crystallize, some of their minerals contain radioactive elements. The radioactive elements that a new rock starts with are called **parent elements**. Soon after the rock hardens, the parent elements begin to change, or decay, into different **daughter elements**. The rate at which a parent element changes into a daughter element is called the **decay rate**. Decay rates are different for different elements. Heating, cooling, or squeezing a rock does not change the decay rate of a particular element.

Decay rates for different elements are measured in a period of time called a half-life. The half-life is defined as the amount of time it takes for half of a parent element to change into a daughter element. For example, saying that the half-life of an element is 100 years means that after 100 years, half of the total amount of the element will have changed into the daughter element and half will remain as the parent. Using this information, the age of a rock can be figured by working backward. By measuring the relative amounts (the ratio) of parent element to daughter element found in a rock sample, scientists can calculate how many half-lives have gone by. Multiplying the number of half-lives by the decay rate produces a date. For example, if you measure the same number of daughter atoms as parent atoms, then you know that one-half of the parent atoms have decayed to the daughter. This tells you that the sample is one half-life, or 100 years, old. If there are three times as many daughter atoms as parent atoms, then the rock is two half-lives, or 200 years, old (after one half-life, you have half of the original atoms; after two half-lives, you have one-quarter of the original parent atoms).

While radioactive age dating is a great tool, it does not work with all rock types, only those where the minerals have

(continues)

Uranium 238 (U238) Radioactive Decay Chain

	Nuclide	Half-life
	uranium—238	4.5×10^9 years
	thorium—234	24.5 days
	protactinium—234	1.14 minutes
	uranium—234	2.33×10^5 years
	thorium—230	8.3×10^4 years
	radium—226	1,590 years
	radon—222	3.825 days
	polonium—218	3.05 minutes
	lead—214	26.8 minutes
	bismuth—214	19.7 minutes
	polonium—214	1.5×10^{-4} seconds
	lead—210	22 years
	bismuth—210	5 days
	polonium—210	140 days
	lead—206	stable

© Infobase Publishing

Figure 3.3 Radioactive age dating is a great tool for figuring out the age of a rock, but works reliably only on igneous and metamorphic rocks.

(continued)

crystallized or re-crystallized from scratch. That means that igneous or metamorphic rocks work well for determining age, but sedimentary rocks give unreliable dates.

ARTHUR HOLMES AND THE CONCEPT OF CONVECTION

Even though his name is not as famous as either James Hutton or Charles Lyell, Arthur Holmes ranks as one of the greatest geologists of all time. He is best known for his textbook *Principles of Physical Geology.* First published in 1944, this book is still used by many geology students today. When it comes to plate tectonic theory, however, Holmes can be thought of as "the man who moved the continents."

Holmes's career as a geologist started soon after his graduation from Imperial College of Science in London in 1910. To help pay his college expenses, he went to work as a prospecting geologist in the country of Mozambique. Unfortunately, he also wound up catching malaria. He returned to England in 1913 just when World War I was starting. As luck would have it, he was too sick to go into the army and fight. Instead, he returned to Imperial College to work as a lab technician and get his Ph.D.

As a graduate student, Holmes read about the work in radioactivity done by Rutherford and Boltwood. He became interested in radioactive dating techniques and, by the end of 1913, he used Boltwood's uranium-lead dating technique to develop the first absolute geologic time scale. For the first time, geologists had actual numbers with which to measure the length of the different geologic periods.

While he was at Imperial College, Holmes had heard about Wegener's book and his theory of continental drift. At the time, he really did not think much about it, preferring to concentrate on better ways of doing radioactive age dating. After receiving his doctorate, Holmes left Imperial College and went to work as a geologist for an oil company. Unfortunately, after a few years, the company went bankrupt, and he returned to England in 1924 in search of a job. His reputation as a top geologist led to his becoming a professor of geology at Durham University. It was here that his interest in Wegener's theory really took off.

Like many geologists of his day, Holmes had been a believer in the idea that mountains formed as a result of Earth contracting when it cooled. After working with so many radioactive elements, however, he realized that this idea was probably wrong for one simple

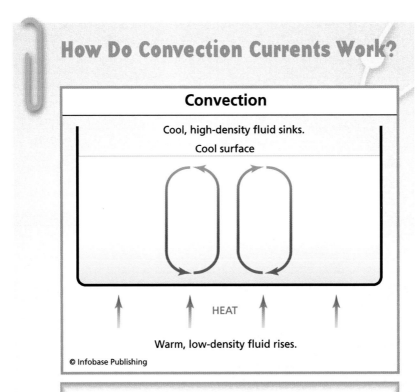

Figure 3.4 The diagram above illustrates how a convection current flows. Most geologists believe convection currents in the Earth's interior make the continents move.

reason: When radioactive elements decay, they also produce heat. Holmes reasoned that the heat from these elements inside Earth would keep the planet from ever cooling completely. If the planet was not cooling, then it could not be contracting, either. To him, continental drift seemed like a more likely answer to the question of where mountains came from.

In 1927, he presented a paper to the Edinburgh Geological Society outlining a new idea. Instead of the continents moving through the rocks of the ocean floor as Wegener had said, Holmes suggested that extremely dense rocks below the outer layer of the Earth were slowly flowing like thick taffy. The continents were like rafts riding along on top of these hot, fluid rocks. He then said that the hot rocks were flowing because of **convection currents** caused by high concentrations of radioactive minerals found inside Earth.

Convection is the process that transfers heat from one place to another by the movement of heated matter. Convection happens most often in fluids like water, air, or magma. As an example of how a convection current works, think of a pot of thick soup cooking on a stove. The heat from the stove causes the soup at the bottom of the pot to heat up first. As the soup at the bottom gets hot, it begins to expand and becomes less dense. It slowly rises to the top of the pot and the cooler soup near the top begins to sink. Once the hot soup reaches the top of the pot, it begins to cool down again, which causes it to contract and become denser. It then begins to sink, replacing new hot soup that is rising. If you watch the soup on the stove, you can actually see this swirling action.

Convection currents happen in many places in nature. Convection currents in the air are what make the wind blow. Convection in the ocean helps to make currents flow. Most geologists believe that convection currents in the Earth are what make the continents move.

By 1930, Holmes had refined his ideas on how convection currents could be the force behind continental drift. He also described how these currents would have caused Pangaea to break up and form the Atlantic Ocean. He published his ideas in an article in a journal called *Transactions of the Geologic Society of Glasgow,* but few people actually read it. When he wrote his groundbreaking textbook in 1944, he devoted an entire chapter to the idea of continental drift. While he noted that the basic concept was possible, he also pointed out many flaws in Wegener's data. After explaining his own ideas about how convection currents could be the driving force behind continental drift, he concluded the chapter with the following statement: "It must be clearly recognized, however, that purely speculative ideas of this kind, specially invented to match the requirements, can have no scientific value until they acquire support from independent evidence."

That independent evidence would come 20 years later from the bottom of the sea and be presented by a scientist named Harry Hammond Hess.

Under the Sea

I f you stop and think about it, the name "Water" would probably be a better name for our planet than "Earth." Dry land, or earth, only makes up about 30% of the planet's surface. Most of the rest is covered by oceans. Up until the mid-twentieth century, little was known about what the seafloors of our planet looked like.

There were several reasons for this lack of information. First and foremost, at certain points past the edge of the continents, the ocean gets really deep! Before the early 1900s, scientists really had no accurate way to measure the ocean's depth. The best method available was to take a line with a weight attached, drop it over the edge of a ship, and see how long it took the weight to reach the bottom. These "soundings," as they were called, worked fine in shallow water, but in the deep ocean, this method encountered real problems. Currents in the water would cause the line to drift in different directions, making it hard to tell when true bottom was reached.

When Alfred Wegener first proposed his continental drift theory, most scientists believed that the deep ocean bottom was simply a flat plain. There were a few clues that this might not be the case, however, such as ocean islands like Hawaii, the Galapagos, and Iceland, which seemed to rise up out of the seafloor. Then, in the late 1800s, the laying of the first undersea telegraph cable from Europe to North America indicated that there was some type of ridge running down the middle of the Atlantic Ocean. The real breakthrough

How Does Sonar Work?

Sonar works on the principle of echolocation, which is the same method that bats and dolphins use to navigate and find food. In active sonar systems, a device called an "acoustic projector" sends out a steady stream of sound waves that move out in all directions. When the sound waves strike an object, they bounce off and reflect back toward the sonar device. The reflected sound waves then

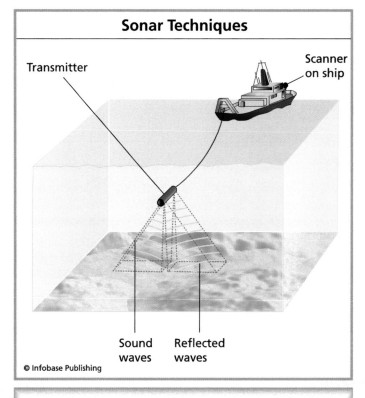

Sonar Techniques

Transmitter

Scanner on ship

Sound waves

Reflected waves

© Infobase Publishing

Figure 4.1   Sonar uses sound waves to measure the depth of the ocean floor. The distance to the seafloor is measured by the time it takes for sound to travel to the seafloor and back to the sound transmitter.

are picked up by a receiver called a hydrophone. Since sound waves travel at a specific speed in seawater, by measuring the time it takes for a wave to travel out and return, a sonar operator can calculate in what direction and how far away an object is. Modern sonar systems are extremely sensitive. Not only can they locate submarines and sunken ships, but they are often used by commercial fishers to find fish. Geologists and oceanographers frequently use sonar to map changes in the seafloor, and a variation of the device is used by doctors in hospitals to take pictures of babies in the womb.

to understanding the true nature of the seafloor surface came during World War I with the development of two new devices: submarines and **sonar**.

Submarines were not a new idea. In fact, the first submarine was built back in the 1620s. However, these early vessels were tiny. They also leaked a great deal and were powered by the use of hand cranks and oars. Nor, before 1900, could submarines dive very deep or stay under water for more than a few hours at a time. Finally, in 1905, German engineers constructed the *Unterseeboot 1*, otherwise known as the "U-boat." This vessel, which was powered by strong diesel engines and electric motors, was the first truly modern submarine.

During the World War I, German U-boats terrorized Allied ships, sank many of them, and caused a great loss of life. While the Allies had submarines of their own, they were not as fast or as maneuverable as the U-boats. The Allies needed an edge against the U-boats, and it came with the invention of sonar.

The word *sonar* is derived from the words "Sound Navigation And Ranging." This device uses sound waves to locate underwater objects. First developed in 1916, sonar systems helped the Allies locate German submarines before they could attack ships. It turns out that sonar was also the perfect answer for scientists who wanted to learn more about what the ocean floor was like.

HARRY HESS UNCOVERS A DEEP-SEA MYSTERY

Even though sonar had been available for more than 20 years, it was not really put to many scientific uses until World War II, when a naval officer named Harry Hess turned an antisubmarine weapon into an important research tool. In the process, he would not only unlock the mystery of what the seafloor looked like, but give the theory of continental drift a whole new look.

Harry Hammond Hess was born in New York City in 1906 and graduated from Yale University with a degree in geology in 1927. After working as an exploration geologist for several years, he entered Princeton University where he received his Ph.D. in 1932. In 1934, he joined the faculty of Princeton, but his teaching career was interrupted in 1941 when he was called into active duty in World War II. Hess was a lieutenant in the naval reserve and eventually he was put in command of a ship called the USS Cape Johnson.

Hess's main duties while in the navy centered on antisubmarine warfare and landing troops on beaches on various islands in the Pacific Ocean. He quickly became an expert in the use of sonar and used it to keep track of the water depth around the islands that he patrolled. He soon realized that sonar would also work in deep water. As Hess and his crew sailed around the Pacific Ocean, he recorded thousands of miles of depth readings, thereby giving scientists their first real look at the ocean floor.

Hess discovered that the ocean floor was not smooth and flat as most scientists had believed, but was full of submerged mountains, valleys, ridges, and unusual flat-topped hills, which he named "guyots" after Arnold Guyot, the founder of the Princeton Department of Geology. After the war, Hess returned to Princeton and continued to conduct research on the geography of the ocean floor.

While Hess was at Princeton, geologist Bruce C. Heezen and cartographer Marie Tharp at Columbia University's Lamont–Doherty Geological Laboratory started to create a picture of the ocean floor that would become much clearer. In 1947, they picked up on the work Hess had started. Heezen, sailing aboard the research vessel *Vema*, began making detailed depth readings in the North Atlantic

Marie Tharp: Pioneering Geologist and Mapmaker Extraordinaire

Marie Tharp was a true pioneer in the field of marine geology. After receiving her degree in English from Ohio University, she attended the University of Michigan where she received her degree in geology. This was a time when few women looked for careers in the Earth sciences, but Marie was a person who liked making new discoveries and was not afraid of working in a "man's job." She started working for an oil company in Oklahoma but then decided to give research a try.

Teaming up with Bruce Heezen at Columbia University gave her the opportunity to become a star in the new field of marine geology. Unfortunately, because she was a woman, she was not allowed to accompany any of the early research cruises that were conducted in the late 1940s and early 1950s. Instead, Heezen went on the cruises and collected the data while Tharp stayed back at Lamont and, from the information that Heezen sent to her, created the maps that would radically

(continues)

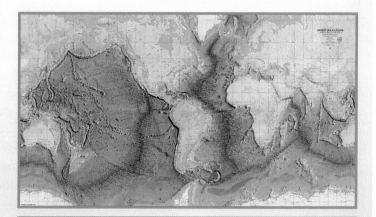

Figure 4.2   Bruce Heezen and Marie Tharp created this world ocean floor panorama.

(continued)

change our view of Earth. Finally, after 33 cruises, the rules were changed and Tharp was able to accompany Heezen out to sea. After Heezen died in 1973, Marie Tharp created her final map. This one showed the entire seafloor of the planet, including all the features that had been discovered. This map, along with the data supplied by several other geologists, would put the theory of plate tectonics on a solid foundation.

Ocean. He supplied the information to Tharp, who then drew the maps. Little by little, a whole new picture of the ocean floor began to emerge.

First, they discovered a mountain chain in the middle of the Atlantic Ocean that runs from near the North Pole, south past Greenland, and almost all the way to Antarctica. From there, this ridge continues east, past southern Africa, through the Indian and Southern Oceans, past Australia and across the Pacific Ocean, and ending near Southern California. In all, this **mid-ocean ridge**, as it has become known, travels over 45,000 miles (80,000 kilometers), making it the longest mountain chain on Earth.

In the center of the mid-ocean ridge is a valley or "rift" lined with active volcanoes. In some places, like Iceland, these volcanoes have risen above the sea. In most places, however, the volcanoes lie under the water, and as they erupt, they add new rock to the surface of the Earth.

In addition to the mid-ocean ridge, Heezen and Tharp's maps also showed deep valleys, many of which run along the edge of the continents. These valleys are known as **submarine trenches**. In many cases, these trenches, which make an almost complete ring around the Pacific Ocean, contain enormous piles of sediment. One other unusual feature on the maps is a series of fractures, or **faults**, that cut across both the ridge and the trenches. Many of these fracture zones would cause the ridge to be offset and split by several hundred kilometers. This led some scientists to wonder if Earth was expanding. It was Harry Hess who came up with another answer and, in the process, solved another great scientific mystery.

THE THEORY OF SEAFLOOR SPREADING

Long before Wegener introduced his ideas of continental drift, geologists had been faced with two other great mysteries of the ocean. First, they wondered what happened to all of the sediment that was carried into the sea by the rivers that emptied into the ocean. Scientists had observed how ponds and lakes would eventually fill in with silt and sand carried in by the streams that flowed into them. If Hutton and Lyell were right about the age of Earth and the fact that processes like erosion and deposition of sediment have been going on for millions of years, then the oceans should be almost filled with sediment. When scientists were finally able to get a close-up look at the seafloor, they found that some sediment covered the bottom, but not nearly enough to account for all the miles of rock that had been eroded off the continents.

The second mystery that puzzled the scientific community was the fact that the ocean contained almost no fossils of creatures that were greater than about 200 million years old. On the continents, however, there were fossils that were three times older and rocks that were close to 4 billion years old. It appeared that the seafloor was much younger than the rest of the planet. If the ocean basins and continents had been in the same positions since Earth first formed, then the rocks from each should be the same age.

Based on his ongoing research, and the maps developed by Heezen and Tharp, Harry Hess thought he knew the answer. He offered a bold new theory to explain it, an idea that has become known as the theory of seafloor spreading. Hess suggested that the ocean floor is like a giant conveyor belt. At the mid-ocean ridges, active volcanoes pump out lava that forms new crust. As the crust is added, the two sides of the seafloor push apart and the ocean gets wider. Along the edges of the continents where the submarine trenches are found, the ocean floor is being consumed. Hess proposed that the trenches are like rips in the surface of the Earth where the old

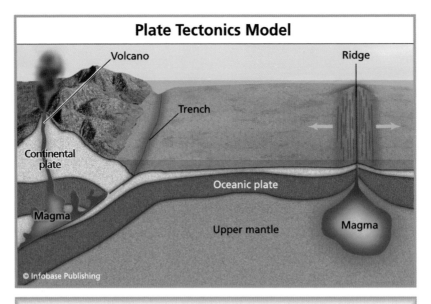

Plate Tectonics Model

Volcano

Ridge

Trench

Continental plate

Oceanic plate

Magma

Upper mantle

Magma

© Infobase Publishing

Figure 4.3 Crust formed at the mid-ocean ridge eventually travels back into the Earth at submarine trenches by a process called subduction.

ocean floor is being forced back down into the Earth by a process called **subduction**. Because the rock that makes up the ocean floor is usually denser than the rocks that make up the continents, the ocean crust will naturally sink underneath the continents.

As the crust sinks, the sediment that was riding on top of the seafloor would get scraped off at these **subduction zones** and plastered onto the edge of the continent, forming mountains along the edge of the coast.

Hess first presented this idea in 1959 but did not formally publish his theory until 1962 in a report entitled *History of Ocean Basins.* The concept was brilliant, and it tied up many geological lose ends. It explained why the rocks and fossils in the ocean were so much younger than the rocks found on the continents. It also explained what happened to all the missing sediment. Most importantly, it gave new life to the idea of continental drift. Seafloor spreading, driven by the convection currents that Arthur Holmes had suggested could be found deep in the Earth, would provide the means to make the continents move. But was there any hard evidence to prove that seafloor spreading existed? It turns out the evidence was already there, frozen in the rocks, and just waiting to be discovered.

EARTH'S PALEOMAGNETIC FIELD

Over two thousand years ago, philosophers in ancient Greece discovered that certain rocks acted like natural magnets. These rocks,

What Produces Earth's Magnetic Field?

Even today, the exact cause of Earth's magnetic field is still somewhat of a mystery. Most geologists believe that it is due to something called the "dynamo effect." It is known that Earth acts like a giant bar magnet with two ends, or "poles." However, scientists are pretty sure that there is not a solid magnet running through the planet. Instead, as Earth rotates, a magnetic field is generated because the center— or **core**—of Earth is thought to be divided into two parts. The **inner core** is believed to be a solid mass made mostly of iron and nickel. The **outer core** is thought to be liquid iron. As Earth spins, the liquid part of the core moves past the solid inner core and it also cuts through the magnetic field of the Sun. Because iron and nickel are good conductors of electricity, this motion generates an electrical current, which in turn generates the planet's magnetic field.

If this sounds complicated, it is. In fact, there are still many questions to be answered. The only thing that we know for sure is that the magnetic field of the planet has two poles that are near the geographic (true north and south) poles of Earth. According to the data derived from ancient rocks, the magnetic field of Earth has completely shut down in the past and the poles have reversed direction. Scientists still have a great deal to learn about how our magnetic field works, but the fact that we have it has helped geologists piece together the plate tectonic puzzle.

which contain the iron-rich mineral magnetite, form from magma that cools and crystallizes. As it cools, iron crystals in the magma line up with Earth's magnetic field. When the rock hardens, these crystals act like little microscopic compass needles pointing to Earth's **north magnetic pole**. This phenomenon is known as **remnant magnetism**, and it has become one of the most important tools used by geologists since the discovery of radioactivity.

In the early 1900s, geologists studying the remnant magnetism of thick sequences of lava flows made an amazing discovery. When they measured the magnetism of the rocks from top to bottom, they found that as they went back in time, the magnetism of the iron crystals reversed direction. It was as though the entire magnetic field of Earth had flipped with the magnetic north pole becoming the magnetic south pole. As they went further back in time, the poles flipped again back to their present-day position.

When this discovery was first announced, most geologists just thought that the findings were due to equipment error. The more rocks they studied, however, the more reversals they found. There was definitely something happening to Earth's magnetic field to make it change over time.

STANLEY RUNCORN DISCOVERS WANDERING POLES

In the 1950s, a number of geologists were trying to make some sense of how Earth's magnetic field works. One of these men was Stanley Runcorn, a geophysicist at the University of Newcastle in England at the time. While measuring the remnant magnetism found frozen into igneous rocks around Europe, he discovered something very strange: It appeared that the position of the north magnetic pole of Earth moved around over time. This was very unexpected. Based on the shape of Earth's magnetic field and the accepted theory of what produced it, the magnetic poles should stay fairly close to the geographic poles. However, according to Runcorn's data, the rocks showed that the north magnetic pole had started out in the Pacific Ocean near Hawaii, then moved over by Japan, and eventually came to rest in its present position in the Arctic.

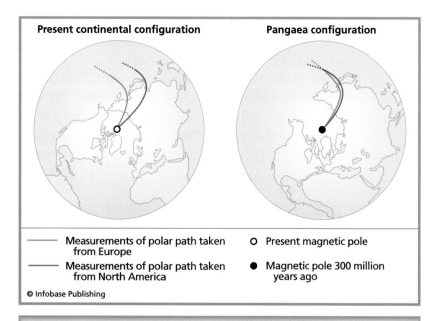

——— Measurements of polar path taken from Europe	○ Present magnetic pole
——— Measurements of polar path taken from North America	● Magnetic pole 300 million years ago

© Infobase Publishing

Figure 4.4   The maps above show the polar wandering curve through Pangaea as well as through the present day configuration, which provides further evidence for moving tectonic plates.

Of course, there was another possibility. Perhaps the north magnetic pole had stayed in one place while the rocks that he was using to measure the magnetism had moved. Runcorn started looking at the paleomagnetic data from other continents and found that these also showed that the magnetic poles had "wandered" in the past. The problem was that the **polar wandering** curves from each of the continents showed that the north magnetic pole had been in different places at the same time in the past. This was impossible. If the magnetic pole had in fact moved, then all of the different curves should have pointed in the same direction. They did not. The only explanation that made sense to Runcorn was that continental drift had moved the rocks into different locations while the pole stayed still.

To test this idea, Runcorn made a map of Pangaea similar to the one that Wegener had drawn 40 years earlier. He then plotted the position of the magnetic poles at different times in the past and, sure enough, when the continents were reassembled, the polar wandering curves matched.

When Runcorn published the results, many scientists thought that his data was flawed. They claimed that because the devices used to measure magnetism in rocks were still very crude, what he thought was a moving pole might just have been an error in the readings. Runcorn pressed on, and as the equipment became better, the data showed that he was on the right track. The final clincher came just a few years later when another group of scientists would use reversals in Earth's magnetic field to prove that the oceans were spreading.

VINE AND MATTHEWS EARN THEIR STRIPES

The 1950s was a busy time for marine geologists. Not only were Bruce Heezen and Marie Tharp creating the first maps of the seafloor, but other scientists were collecting data on the remnant magnetism of the rocks that were found on the bottom of the ocean. It was during this time that Arthur Raff and Ronald Mason made a fascinating discovery. The two men were conducting a magnetic survey of the Pacific Ocean seafloor off the coast of Oregon. As they sailed back and forth across the mid-ocean ridge, they found that the ocean bottom showed some very unusual magnetic properties. In some places, the magnetic field was stronger than normal, while other locations showed it to be weaker than normal. Called **magnetic anomalies**, these features took the form of long, narrow strips that ran parallel to the mid-ocean ridge across the seafloor.

At first, Raff and Mason did not know what to make of these "magnetic stripes," but they published their findings in 1961 anyway. The paper caught the attention of two geologists working in England. Drummond Matthews was a geophysicist working at Cambridge University who, along with a graduate student named Frederick Vine, had been studying events called **magnetic reversals**. During these periods, it appeared that Earth's magnetic field had totally

Figure 4.5 At right is an illustration of the magnetic "striping" in the seafloor. As the magnetic orientation of the Earth switches over millions of years, the magnetic particles in the ocean point toward whichever pole is the magnetic north at the time that the new crust is formed.

Magnetism in the Seafloor

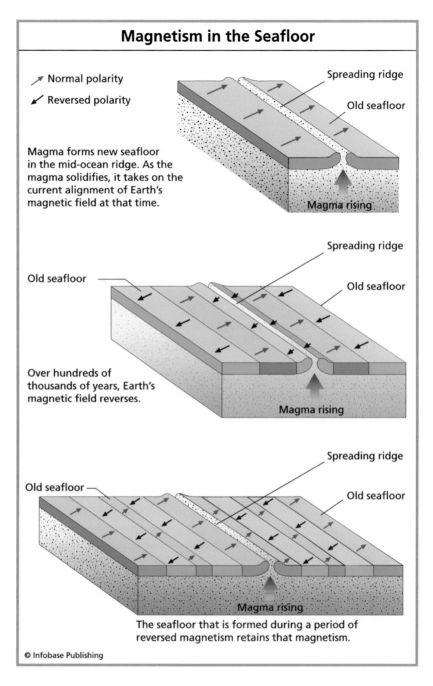

↗ Normal polarity

↙ Reversed polarity

Magma forms new seafloor in the mid-ocean ridge. As the magma solidifies, it takes on the current alignment of Earth's magnetic field at that time.

Spreading ridge

Old seafloor

Magma rising

Spreading ridge

Old seafloor

Old seafloor

Over hundreds of thousands of years, Earth's magnetic field reverses.

Magma rising

Spreading ridge

Old seafloor

Old seafloor

Magma rising

The seafloor that is formed during a period of reversed magnetism retains that magnetism.

© Infobase Publishing

flipped, with the north magnetic pole becoming the south pole and vice versa. Vine and Matthews had been looking at data from the Indian Ocean that showed a similar pattern to the one reported by

Raff and Mason. They thought that the two sets of data had to be linked some way.

In both cases, the magnetic stripes were centered on the mid-ocean ridges. They also noted that the stripes were not of even thicknesses. Some were fairly narrow and some were quite thick, so when they were viewed as a group, the stripes made a very distinctive pattern, almost like the bar code that we use on packages today. When Vine and Matthews looked at the stripe pattern on one side of the mid-ocean ridge, they found that it was almost identical to the pattern on the other side, except reversed. It was like the two sets of stripes were mirror images of each other.

After studying the problem, Vine and Matthews came up with a radical idea to explain the origins of the magnetic stripes. They asked a simple question: What if the magnetic anomalies were really caused by past magnetic reversals that were preserved in the ocean rocks? In places where the anomaly was stronger, the rocks matched the present-day magnetic field. In places where the anomaly was weaker, the rocks were formed when Earth 's magnetic field was reversed. They then explained that the reason the patterns of magnetic stripes formed a mirror image across the mid-ocean ridge was due to the fact that this is where new seafloor was being produced. As fresh lava flowed out of the ridge, it would push the old seafloor out in opposite directions.

Vine and Matthews published their theory in 1963, right after Hess published his theory about seafloor spreading. The two theories fit together perfectly. At first, many geologists were skeptical about this bold idea because the amount of data to support it was limited. Also, there were still many questions about the accuracy of the magnetic anomalies. As new data came in, it started to look like they were on to something.

The real clincher came in the late 1960s, when geologists began getting radioactive age dates for the rocks at the bottom of the ocean. Drilling into the seafloor produced samples that clearly showed that the rocks near the ridge were very young. As they brought up more samples from the ridge going out in either direction, the scientists found that the seafloor got older, with the oldest rocks being found farthest from the ridge. In 1965, Vine published another paper with Canadian geologist J. Tuzo Wilson.

Their data all but confirmed that Hess's theory of seafloor spreading was correct.

By the mid-1960s, the evidence to support the idea of continental drift was overwhelming. Magnetic stripes and age dates from the ocean coupled with the polar wandering data from the land left little doubt that the continents had moved. Even though most geologists were convinced that Earth's surface was shifting, they were still at a loss to explain how it all worked. What was needed was a better understanding of what was happening deep inside the planet. All the information was there waiting to be discovered. What was needed was a way to see it.

5

Getting the Inside Story

At the start of the twentieth century, the discovery of radioactivity was not the only development to help geologists unravel the history of the planet. Scientists who were studying **earthquakes** at this time were finding out just how important these shocking events could be.

Earthquakes have been recorded in history for thousands of years. When an earthquake strikes, the ground suddenly starts shaking without any warning and then stops just as quickly. Most earthquakes last less than a minute, but the damage they do can take a lifetime to repair. While some earthquakes are quite violent, most are pretty tame. In fact, hundreds of earthquakes occur every day that are not even felt. But those quakes that are felt, the "big ones," are the ones that worry scientists and engineers. The worst damage from these earthquakes often comes when their vibrations cause buildings to collapse, trapping and killing the people inside.

In ancient times, most people believed that earthquakes were a sign from God, who was angry with people. They believed that the only way to stop an earthquake was to repent or offer sacrifices. As time went on, scientists started realizing that earthquakes did not happen everywhere but seemed to occur only in certain locations. They also realized that earthquakes, like lightning and volcanic eruptions, were not due to angry gods, but were acts of nature.

In order to understand earthquakes better, scientists built devices called *seismographs*. These special instruments record when an earthquake happens and measure how strong it is. The first seismographs were very crude, but by the late 1800s, their technology improved to where scientists could analyze earthquake vibrations. This led to a whole new area of geology called **seismology**. **Seismologists** discovered that earthquakes actually produce several different types of vibrations called **seismic waves**. Each type of wave has its own special properties.

When an earthquake rumbles, the ground shifts deep under the surface. This shifting releases a series of seismic waves that travel through the ground. The fastest waves are called **P-waves**, which stands for *primary wave*. These are the first waves to arrive at a seismograph after an earthquake happens. The second waves to arrive

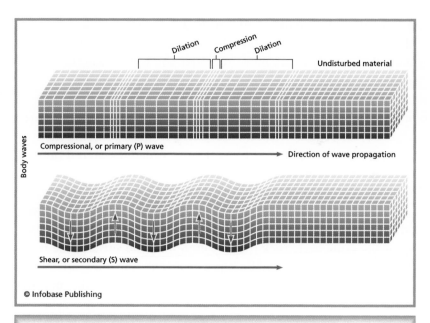

Figure 5.1 Primary and secondary seismic waves move through material in different ways.

are called **S-waves** (secondary waves), which are also called "shear waves." P-waves can move through liquids like water and magma, but S-waves can only move through solid rock.

By the early twentieth century, seismologists had learned a great deal about earthquakes from studying their waves. They discovered that some earthquakes take place deep underground, while others are fairly shallow. They named the point where Earth actually shifts the **focus**. The point on the ground surface directly above the focus of an earthquake was called the **epicenter**. By recording the difference in arrival times between P- and S-waves, scientists could calculate the distance to an earthquake epicenter from the seismograph that recorded the waves. Using data from three different seismographs allowed them to pinpoint the location of the epicenter.

One of the most important discoveries made by seismologists was the fact that seismic waves, like light and sound waves, could bend and bounce when they hit rock with different properties. By plotting the way that waves moved through the Earth, seismologists could get an idea what the rocks looked like below the surface without having to dig or drill. This was the key that geologists were looking for. At the start of the twentieth century, geologists finally could piece together the inner structure of the planet.

By the early part of the twentieth century, geologists had set up hundreds of seismographs around the world. These devices were so sensitive, they could detect the vibrations from large earthquakes on the opposite side of the Earth. As they recorded the arrival times of seismic waves from different earthquake events, seismologists soon discovered a problem. Based on earlier studies of how fast these waves traveled through rocks, the times they were getting were way off the predicted numbers. If Earth was a solid, uniform planet made up of the same basic rock that is found near the surface, the travel times for the waves should be very consistent. The only explanation for these variations in speed was that Earth was not a solid, uniform planet.

By the mid-1900s, a number of geologists, including Charles Richter (for whom the Richter Scale is named) and Beno Gutenberg in the United States and Harold Jeffreys in England, were tackling

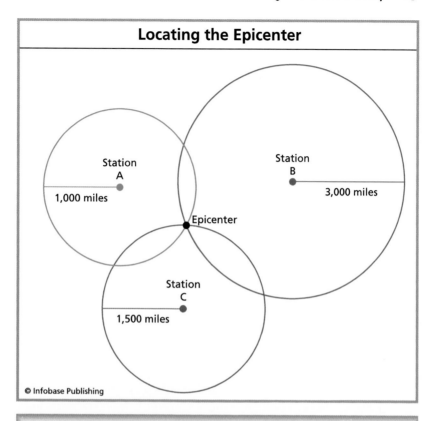

Locating the Epicenter

Station A

1,000 miles

Station B

3,000 miles

Epicenter

Station C

1,500 miles

© Infobase Publishing

Figure 5.2 Scientists are able to locate an earthquake's epicenter using data from three different seismic stations. Each center determines a radius where the epicenter might be located. The intersection of the three centers' radii is the location of the epicenter.

the problem. They found that Earth is really made up of different layers. The heaviest, densest materials lie at the center of the planet, and lighter materials are near the surface. In 1952, an American geologist named Albert Francis Birch published a paper that put all these pieces together.

By studying many lines of evidence, Birch concluded that Earth is really made up of four distinct layers. At the center of the planet is a dense, solid inner core made of mostly iron and nickel. This inner core is surrounded by a second outer core that is made of a liquid metal. As mentioned earlier, it is the interaction of these

Charles Richter Invents a Scale

When it comes to earthquakes, many people have heard of the Richter Scale but few know much about the man who developed it, Charles Francis Richter. Charles Richter was born in 1900 on a farm in Ohio. After his parents divorced, he and his mother moved to California, a part of the world known for its many earthquakes. In 1920, he graduated from Stanford University, eventually receiving his Ph.D. in theoretical physics from the California Institute of Technology (Cal Tech) in 1928. A year earlier, Richter had started working at the Carnegie Institution of Washington's Seismological Laboratory in Pasadena, California, where he met Beno Gutenberg, a seismologist who worked at the lab at the time.

Richter's research centered on the actual physics involved in earthquakes. He and Gutenberg measured the energy output of local earthquakes to see if they could come up with a way of classifying them. At the time, the only way of ranking earthquakes was a system developed by an Italian scientist named Giuseppe Mercalli back in 1902. The Mercalli scale was based on observations of damage to buildings at different locations near an earthquake epicenter. However, the problem with this scale was that the same earthquake could give very different Mercalli measurements at two different locations. What

two parts of the core that is thought to produce Earth's magnetic field.

Surrounding the core is the bulk of the planet called the **mantle**. The mantle is thought to be composed of dense rocks that are under such high pressure that they actually flow like liquids over long periods of time. Finally, sitting on top of the mantle is a relatively thin, brittle layer of rock called the **crust**. In 1910, a Croatian seismologist named Andrija Mohorovicic used the refraction, or bending, of seismic waves to discover the crust-mantle bound-

was needed was a standard way to measure the energy output of the earthquake itself.

After cataloging the seismograms of dozens of earthquakes, Richter and Gutenberg came up with an idea. By using the height of the S-waves recorded on a seismogram, they were able to come up with a way to measure the intensity of an earthquake. Richter developed a logarithmic magnitude scale where each whole number on the scale would represent a 10-fold increase in the amplitude of height of the wave recorded on a seismogram. Richter and Gutenberg published their work in 1935, but even though both men shared in the development of the scale, only Richter's name was given to it.

In 1936, Richter was asked to head up the newly formed Seismological Laboratory at the California Institute of Technology where he also started teaching. He would remain at Cal Tech for the next 35 years, teaching and conducting research. During this time, Richter wrote several classic textbooks dealing with earthquakes, including *Elementary Seismology*, which was published in 1958 and is still used today. After he retired in 1970, Richter continued to work as a media consultant. He died in 1985, four days after his 85th birthday. His name will always be remembered every time an earthquake is measured.

ary and, in the process, helped explain where earthquakes come from.

PEELING BACK THE CRUST

After Mohorovicic made his discovery, geologists began taking a closer look at the composition of Earth's crust. They found that the crust is not one uniform layer. Instead, there are many important

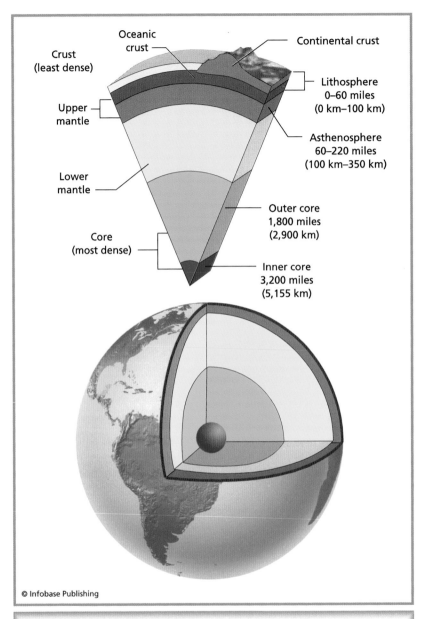

Figure 5.3 The Earth is made up of layers of varying depth.

differences between the crust that lies under the oceans and the crust that makes up the continents. The most obvious difference has to do with the thickness of the two. While the average thickness of

Inge Lehmann Gets to the Core of the Matter

In the early 1900s, the science of seismology was considered a "man's field." Yet one of most important discoveries ever made about the composition of our planet was made by a woman. Inge Lehmann was a Danish scientist who refused to be stopped because of her gender. Born in 1888, Lehmann attended the first coeducational school in Denmark. Here, boys and girls were taught the same subjects and treated as equals. This was quite rare in those days. Because of her strong desire to learn and the fact that she had this unusual early education, Inge was not afraid to take on the male-dominated world of science when she became an adult.

In 1920, she earned her master's degree in mathematics from the University of Copenhagen. After several years of work during which she used her training in mathematics, Lehmann changed careers and began working with a scientist named N.E. Norlund. Norlund was setting up a series of seismic monitoring stations throughout Greenland and northern Europe, and Lehmann was delighted by the idea of traveling while working. She quickly became an expert at reading seismograms and soon returned to the University of Copenhagen to study seismology. After receiving a second master's degree, Lehmann was named chief of the seismology department of the newly created Royal Danish Geodetic Institute in 1928. Here she recorded hundreds of seismograms and published regular seismic bulletins.

While studying the seismograms of deep focus earthquakes, Lehmann noticed a pattern. Some of the P-waves that should have been bent as they passed through Earth's core seemed to be bouncing off of something

(continues)

(continued)

instead. Lehmann analyzed the problem further and concluded that this type of wave motion could only happen if Earth's core was really made up of two layers. Instead of having a single, large, solid core, Lehmann suggested that Earth has a liquid outer core surrounding a smaller solid inner core. She published her findings in a paper simply called "P′" ("P prime") in 1936. At first, few geologists accepted the idea of a double core, but as new data became available, it was clear that Lehmann was correct.

Lehmann continued working in the Danish Geodetic Institute until 1953, at which point she traveled to other labs around the world. In the United States, she conducted research at both the Lamont-Doherty Earth Observatory and the seismological lab at Cal Tech. In 1964, she received a Ph.D. from Columbia University. In 1971, the American Geophysical Union awarded her their highest honor, the William Bowie Medal. Inge Lehmann died in 1993, two months short of her 105th birthday. In 1997, the American Geophysical Union established the Lehmann Medal in her honor, but her greatest prize has to be the name given to the boundary between Earth's inner and outer core: the Lehmann Discontinuity.

the crust in the ocean is only about 3 miles (5 km), the continental crust is often found to be 18 to 25 miles (30 to 40 km) thick. In fact, under high mountains, the continental crust can be as much as 40 miles (65 km) thick, or more than 10 times thicker than the oceanic crust.

Another important difference between the oceanic and continental crust has to do with their individual composition. The crust under the continents appears to be made up of two distinct layers. The top layer is rich in the elements silica and aluminum and is often called the **sial** (derived from the first letters of silica and aluminum).

Got His Moho Working

Andrija Mohorovicic was born in Volosko, Croatia, in 1857. The son of a carpenter, young Andrija showed his brilliance at an early age. By the time he was 15, he could speak 4 languages and was a whiz in math. After graduating from the University of Prague with a degree in physics and mathematics, he returned to Croatia and spent seven years teaching Earth and physical sciences at a high school. In 1882, he became a member of the faculty at the Nautical School in Bakar, Croatia, where his research interests took hold.

While at the Nautical School, Mohorovicic taught oceanography and meteorology. Like Wegener, he became fascinated with changes in the weather and climate, and he established a meteorological station at the school. He became so good at recording data that, in 1892, he became the head of the national meteorological observatory in Zagreb. In this new position, he was able to obtain better scientific instruments, including seismographs for recording earthquake data. Mohorovicic became fascinated with earthquakes and quickly became an expert in interpreting seismic data.

After a particularly large earthquake hit Europe in October 1909, he gathered seismograms from all around the region. After doing a detailed analysis of the wave patterns from many different seismic recordings, he made his most important discovery. Mohorovicic was able to show that there was a sudden change in density between the surface rocks and those located several miles below. He had discovered the boundary between the crust and the mantle! In honor of this achievement, this boundary is now called the "Mohorovicic Discontinuity" or **Moho** for short. As we will see a little later on, the Moho plays a major role in the movement of Earth's crust. Its discovery was another important piece in the plate tectonic puzzle.

The lower section of the crust has some silica, but it is also rich in the element magnesium and is called **sima** (*si* and *ma*). Because it is thinner, the crust under the ocean is made up of just a single layer of sima.

These differences in composition mean that rocks on land are much more variable than oceanic rock. For the most part, the rock on the seafloor is made of an igneous rock called basalt. Basalt contains a great deal of heavy elements like iron and magnesium. As a result, basalts tend to have a high density. Continental rocks, on the other hand, can be igneous, metamorphic, or sedimentary. For the most part, continental rocks have a much lower density than the basalts of the ocean. This difference in density plays an important role in how and why the continents move.

EARTHQUAKES AND VOLCANOES DRAW SOME LINES

One of the most important things that geologists discovered when they conducted seismic studies of the crust was that it was not made up of one single piece. Instead, the crust is cracked and broken into many different pieces. Scientists discovered this fact as they began to learn more about the causes of earthquakes. It had long been known that earthquakes do not happen with the same frequency all over the planet. Some places, like California and Mexico, have many earthquakes. Places like Michigan and Maine have relatively few. The big question that geologists had to answer was why this should be. To understand the problem, it helps to understand what causes an earthquake in the first place.

During an earthquake, forces inside the planet cause two pieces of the crust to move past each other. The breaks between the pieces of crust are called faults, and they come in many different sizes. As might be expected, large earthquakes usually happen at big faults and small quakes usually happen at small ones. In the early 1960s, several geologists began taking the really simple approach of plotting the location of earthquakes on a map of the world. In a short time, an interesting picture began to develop.

Figure 5.4 Volcanoes (red triangles) and major earthquakes (yellow dots) are concentrated along the boundaries of tectonic plates (red lines).

It seems that most earthquakes occur in the ocean along narrow bands. The single biggest concentration of them can be found in a broad ring that roughly circles the Pacific Ocean. Another area of earthquake concentration is found along the mid-ocean ridges. Earthquakes that occur on land are usually found in mountainous regions.

After geologists plotted the earthquake locations, they did the same for active volcanoes. Volcanoes are openings in the Earth where hot liquid magma rises to the surface from deep within.

The Ring of Fire

So many active volcanoes are located around the rim of the Pacific Ocean that geologists have nicknamed it the "Ring of Fire." While all volcanoes are dangerous, the size and explosiveness of most of the volcanoes found in this ring make them particularly hazardous. In recent years, eruptions at Mount St. Helens in the United States and Mount Pinatubo in the Philippines have been responsible for the destruction of a tremendous amount of property and loss of life.

These eruptions are small compared to past eruptions, however. In 1883, Krakatau, located between the islands of Java and Sumatra, blew up with such force that it was heard in Australia, over 2,000 miles (3,219 km) away. An even bigger eruption had occurred earlier, in Indonesia in 1815, when the entire top of Mount Tambora blew off, killing over 50,000 people. More, possibly bigger, problems with the volcanoes in the Ring of Fire lie in the future. Many of the Ring of Fire volcanoes are among the world's largest, including Mount Fuji in Japan and Mount Rainier in the United States, both of which are just waiting to blow. Because the populations surrounding these volcanoes are so large, their eruptions could impact millions of people.

Table 5-1: Deadly Volcanoes in the Ring of Fire		
Year	Volcano Name and Location	Estimated Number Killed
1792	Unzen, Japan	15,000
1815	Tambora, Indonesia	92,000
1883	Krakatau, Indonesia	36,400
1980	Mount St. Helens, U.S.A.	57
1991	Pinatubo, Philippines	932

When the earthquake map was laid on top of the volcano map, they matched up very closely: The areas that had the highest concentration of earthquakes also had the highest concentration of active volcanoes. This was not simply a coincidence. Earthquakes and volcanoes show up in the same places because they are connected.

SUBDUCTION ZONES: WHAT COMES UP MUST GO DOWN

Harry Hess's theory of seafloor spreading described how new ocean crust was created at the mid-ocean ridges and was consumed in the seafloor trenches or along the edges of continents. While this seemed like a logical idea, there was little data to support it when it was first proposed. But as geologists gathered additional information about the crust from volcanoes and earthquakes, Hess's ideas began to look better and better.

High concentrations of earthquakes and volcanoes along the mid-ocean ridges clearly supported the idea that magma created new ocean crust as it flowed out of the Earth along these features. The question was, did earthquakes and volcanoes offer any evidence to suggest that subduction was also happening? The answer was a resounding yes.

Almost as soon as seismologists started recording data from earthquakes, they discovered that most of them had a shallow focus. This meant that the point of motion was not very far below the surface, usually less than 6 miles (10 km). Every so often they would record an earthquake that had a focus that was deeper than 62 miles (100 km).

When seismologists plotted these "deep focus" earthquakes on a map, they discovered that they only occurred under ocean trenches or along the edges of continents where tall mountains and active volcanoes were located. In other words, deep focus earthquakes only happened in areas that Hess had said were subduction zones. The most logical explanation was that deep focus earthquakes were triggered by pieces of old ocean crust that were sinking back down into the Earth to be recycled. If this were truly the case, it would also explain the mountains and volcanoes. As one piece of crust slid under the other, the surface would be bent up to create the mountains. The enormous friction caused by pieces of the crust rubbing against each other would melt some of the rock to create the magma that would then flow to the surface to form volcanoes.

FINDING THE ASTHENOSPHERE

By the late 1960s, the plate tectonic puzzle was almost complete. Almost all the pieces were in place to support a bold new theory of how the surface of Earth constantly changes. Only one last question remained to be answered: How could pieces of the crust move about if the rocks of the mantle were solid? The answer was obvious—maybe the mantle isn't so solid after all.

Seismologists conducting research on the speed of seismic waves moving through Earth generally found that the deeper the waves went, the faster they moved. For some reason, though, there was a zone between 65 and 210 miles (100 and 350 km) below the surface where both P- and S-waves slowed down. This "low-velocity zone" did not make sense because the density and composition of the rocks in this area appeared to be similar to those found above and below it. The only other explanation for this drop in wave speed was that the rocks in this zone were not as solid as those surrounding it. In fact, seismic velocities in this zone were so low that in some places the rock seemed to behave like a super-thick fluid.

Scientists named this area the **asthenosphere** to distinguish it from the area of the mantle above and below it. They now believe that the asthenosphere behaves like a fluid because of pockets of basaltic magma spread throughout the solid rock. This magma is thought to be the source of the new crust that forms in the mid-ocean ridges. It is also thought to be the layer on which the continents "float" as they move around the Earth. With the discovery of the asthenosphere, all geologists had to do was fit all the pieces together. Once this was done, the theory of plate tectonics was finally born.

Putting Plate Tectonic Theory to the Test

Even though it may seem like the theory of plate tectonics is simply a new and improved version of Wegener's continental drift hypothesis, the two ideas are really quite different. While both theories feature moving landmasses, to say the two are equal would be like comparing the Wright brothers' first airplane with a modern military jet. Unlike the original idea of continental drift, modern plate tectonic theory not only states that the continents were once one single landmass, it also explains in great detail how this landmass broke up and why the continents keep moving today. Most importantly, plate tectonics has answered a number of other questions that had been troubling geologists and has brought together different areas of science under one umbrella. Even though it is a relatively new theory, plate tectonics has stood the "test of time."

PLATE TECTONICS OFFERS SOME NEW GEOLOGICAL EXPLANATIONS

When the theory that we now call "plate tectonics" was finally put together in the late 1960s, many scientists had a hand in it. In 1967, two geologists named Dan McKenzie and Robert Parker published a paper in the journal *Nature* that described seismic activity in the area around the Pacific Ocean. These scientists were the first ones to use the term "plate tectonics" in print.

The theory of plate tectonics states that the surface of Earth is made up of about eight large and about a dozen small "chunks" called **tectonic plates**. These plates are between 30 and 90 miles (50 to 150 km) thick. Taken together, they make up the **lithosphere**, which is the outermost layer of the planet. The lithosphere is made up of rocks from both the crust and the upper mantle. The oceans and the continents we see at the surface are simply riding on the plates below. Some plates, like the one under the Pacific Ocean, just carry oceanic crust. Other plates, like the one under North America, carry both oceanic and continental crust. The plates of the lithosphere move by sliding on top of the semisolid rocks of the asthenosphere below.

Plate boundaries are areas with a large amount of earthquake and volcanic activity. The central areas of tectonic plates are fairly inactive and have very few active volcanoes or earthquakes. Three different types of boundaries separate tectonic plates. A **divergent boundary** is where two plates are being pushed apart. Divergent boundaries are commonly found at mid-ocean ridges where magma is flowing to the surface to form new oceanic crust. A **convergent boundary**, on the other hand, is where two plates are coming together. Convergent boundaries are where the process of subduction takes place. These can be found at deep ocean trenches or alongside continents. Most mountains form at either convergent or divergent boundaries.

The last type of boundary is a place where new crust does not form and old crust is not destroyed. At these so-called "neutral boundaries," plates just slide past each other. One of the most famous neutral boundaries is found at the San Andreas fault along the West Coast of the United States where the Pacific plate and the North American plate scrape past each other, triggering lots of earthquakes. Other neutral boundaries occur in the middle of the ocean and appear as **transform faults**, which cut across mid-ocean ridges and trenches.

SEEING THE PAST IN PRESENT EVENTS

Even though the theory of plate tectonics had many supporters when it was finally introduced, there were still a great many scientists who

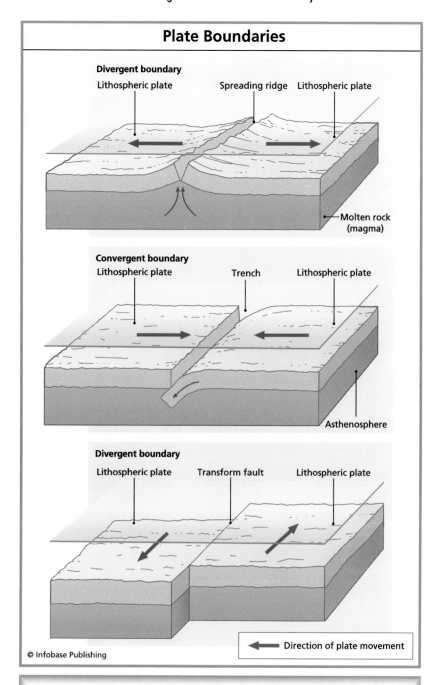

Plate Boundaries

Divergent boundary

Lithospheric plate   Spreading ridge   Lithospheric plate

Molten rock (magma)

Convergent boundary

Lithospheric plate   Trench   Lithospheric plate

Asthenosphere

Divergent boundary

Lithospheric plate   Transform fault   Lithospheric plate

Direction of plate movement

© Infobase Publishing

Figure 6.1 Examples of divergent *(top)*, convergent *(middle)*, and transform *(bottom)* plate boundaries

J. Tuzo Wilson: Champion of the Theory

John Tuzo Wilson was a Canadian geologist who graduated from the University of Toronto in 1930 with a degree in geophysical studies. He received his Ph.D. from Princeton University in 1936 and went to work for the Geological Survey of Canada. During World War II, he served with the Royal Canadian Engineers. When the war ended, he returned to the University of Toronto, where he became a professor of geophysics.

In the late 1950s and early 1960s, Wilson followed the research of Hess, Heezen, and others and became an outspoken supporter of seafloor spreading. One of the questions that interested him the most concerned the unusual faults that cut across the mid-ocean ridges and trenches. Most geologists believed that these "transform faults" happened after the ridges had formed, but Wilson disagreed. He believed that the transform faults had always been part of the ocean crust and that the crust itself simply moved as a solid, unbroken piece. He used the term "plate" to describe large sections of Earth's crust and suggested that the entire surface of Earth was made up of about two dozen plates of different sizes.

Within a few years, earthquake data collected along these areas showed that Wilson was right. The center areas of plates had very few earthquakes, while plate boundaries were extremely active. His work on transform faults provided the missing piece in Hess's theory of seafloor spreading, and it directly led to the development of the theory of plate tectonics.

were skeptical. These doubters were eager to put the theory to the test. One of the first questions they had concerned the age of the crust. Radioactive age dates from the continents showed that Earth was at least 4 billion years old. The oldest crust in the ocean does not appear to be more than 200 million years old. Were there any oceans before the breakup of Pangaea? If so, what happened to the missing crust?

According to plate tectonic theory, any ocean crust that existed before the breakup of Pangaea would have either been recycled back into the mantle or have been plastered onto the side of a continent. The evidence to support this can be seen in the presence of the many numerous marine fossils dating back over 500 million years ago that can be found high in the mountains along the edge of continents, right where they should be if two plates had collided.

The question is, if ocean crust keeps getting recycled, why does the same process not happen with continental crust? The answer is related to the relative density of the two types of crust. Since ocean crust is made of heavier elements (or sima), it is denser and will easily subduct under the less dense continental crust (or sial). Also, the oceanic crust is thinner, so it offers less resistance to subduction than the continental crust. When two plates containing continental crust collide, instead of one subducting under the other, they both rise up. This is exactly what can be seen happening in the Himalayan mountains today. In fact, based on recent surveys, it appears that many of the mountains of the Himalayas are still getting taller. It also explains how many inland mountain chains such as the Appalachians and the Alps were created. Both of these mountain chains were located in areas that were caught between two pieces of continental crust that had collided in the distant past.

One of the most important features of plate tectonic theory is that the continents have not always looked the way they do today. Based on the reconstructions done by Wegener and others, most geologists agree that all the continents were joined about 200 million years ago in a single mass called Pangaea. The best reconstruction of this great continent was published in 1965 by Edward Bullard of Cambridge University in England.

Using a computer (which was a very new device at the time) and data supplied by undersea maps, Bullard did something very clever: Rather than fit the continents back together along their coastlines, he fit them together along the continental shelves. Continental shelves are really extensions of the continents into the oceans that lie under shallow water. This new "Bullard fit" removed many of the gaps that were present in Wegener's original map of Pangaea. It left little doubt that the continents had been joined together in a single landmass.

Before there was a Pangaea, however, the continents were again separated. The shapes of those earlier continents did not look like the present-day continents though. Geologists are still trying to work out the continental reconstructions from these earlier times, but there does seem to be some type of cycle at work. Every 250 million years or so, for some reason, it appears that the continents separate and then rejoin in a different pattern. One thing that is known for sure is that the process of continents joining together and separating is happening today, because we can see it in action. One area that has geologists' attention is the Red Sea and the Gulf of Aden. This area is known as a *rift zone*, and it is an active spreading center. Given enough time, the Red Sea may become an ocean as wide as the Atlantic.

MANY QUESTIONS STILL REMAIN

Even though plate tectonics has answered many of the questions dealing with how the surface of Earth changes over time, the theory itself still has many unanswered questions. Perhaps the biggest question is also the simplest one: What makes the tectonic plates move in the first place? The most common answer goes back to Arthur Holmes's idea of convection currents. If you recall, Holmes believed that heat generated by radioactive elements would cause "hot spots" in the mantle. As the rock became hotter, its density would decrease and it would start to rise. If this idea is correct, then convection currents in the asthenosphere would literally push the plates along. In places where two convection cells moved apart, there would be a divergent plate boundary, such as a mid-ocean ridge. In places where two convection cells came together, there would be a convergent plate boundary.

There are a few problems with having convection currents drive plate tectonics, though. If you recall, convection is how heat moves through fluids, like liquid and gas. Convection does not usually occur in solids. Seismic data shows that the asthenosphere

Plate Tectonics Helps Other Scientists Make New Discoveries

Plate tectonic theory has not only helped geologists answer questions about the structure of our Earth, it also has made contributions to other fields. Reconstructions of past continents have helped scientists in the fields of climatology and biology solve some of their own mysteries.

One example relates to the way that moving continents have changed the circulation pattern of ocean currents. When Pangaea began breaking up, water in the ocean was free to circulate around the planet at the equator. This made Earth somewhat warmer than today because warm ocean water could travel around the globe freely. But after the Atlantic Ocean opened up, the circulation pattern began to change. When the connection between North and South America, including Central America, was made about 2 million years ago, the equatorial circulation was blocked. Water then

(continues)

Figure 6.2   The platypus *(left)* and the echidna *(right)* are both monotremes, the only mammals in the world that lay eggs instead of giving live birth.

(continued)

circulated in the Atlantic from pole to pole instead of around the equator. This had a chilling effect on Earth. Some scientists believe this small change is what triggered the last ice age.

Plate tectonics has also played a huge role in explaining the evolutionary history of many animal and plant species scattered throughout the world. Take Australia for instance. It is well known that the "land down under" is home to some interesting animals like the echidna and the duck-billed platypus. These animals belong to a group of mammals called *monotremes* that are quite primitive and still lay eggs. In all other parts of the world, monotremes have been replaced by placental mammals, which produce young through live birth. Most biologists believe that the live birth process is much more efficient than laying eggs. So far, monotremes have only been found in Australia and some of the surrounding islands like Tasmania. The reason for the existence of these unusual animals is related to the theory of plate tectonics. According to the theory, when Gondwanaland broke up, Australia was the first to separate from the rest of the continents. This caused the primitive animals found there to become isolated from the rest of the mammals in the world. This separation prevented them from following the same evolutionary pathways that the mammals in the rest of the world followed.

is in a semisolid state. There is no proof that convection currents can form in a solid, even one as soft and pliable as the rocks in the asthenosphere. An even bigger problem concerns how the plates move on the asthenosphere. If the plates are simply sliding over the rocks of the asthenosphere, then the motion has to happen below it. Based on the seismic data, it appears that the mantle below the asthenosphere is a true solid, meaning that convection would not be possible there.

Even if convection is the cause of plate motion, then there is the question of why the motion starts, stops, and reverses direction. It is fairly certain that when two plates that carry continental crust collide, the motion between them is slowed because of the enormous forces needed to push the rocks up to form mountains. This may provide part of the answer. When the resisting force gets to be too great in one direction, the motion simply changes direction. As of yet, there is no proof that this occurs, but many geologists continue to explore this question.

Clearly, the theory of plate tectonics is far from complete. Geologists still have a great deal of work to do. In many cases, just when they think they have all the questions answered, a whole bunch of new questions arise. Remember, it took over 50 years for modern plate tectonic theory to come together. In many cases, the answers

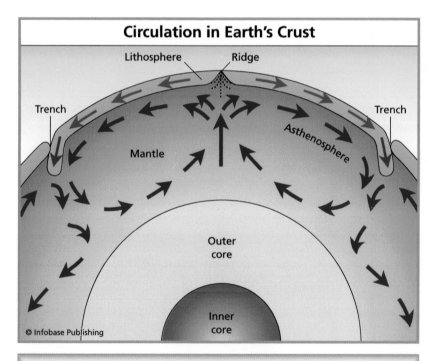

Figure 6.3 Convection cells might drive plate tectonics at converging and diverging boundaries.

had to wait for new technology to be developed. At the present time, plate tectonics is the best way that scientists have to explain the way the surface of our planet behaves. Who knows if, in another 50 years, an entirely new theory may come along to replace it. But that is the beauty of science—the only thing for certain is that it keeps changing!

Glossary

Absolute Time   A time scale based on the radioactive decay of certain elements that presents time periods in years.

Asthenosphere   The part of the mantle that slows down earthquake waves. It is thought to be the layer on which the tectonic plates move.

Basalt   An igneous rock that is rich in iron and makes up most of the seafloor.

Catastrophism   The idea that large-scale Earth changes can only happen during large catastrophic events.

Continental drift   The theory developed by Alfred Wegener in the early 1900s that says that the continents have changed their positions over time.

Convection   The process where heat is transferred through a fluid.

Convection current   The circular path that a fluid takes when it is heated from below.

Convergent boundary   The area where two tectonic plates collide.

Core   The center of the Earth. Earth's core has two parts: a solid inner core and a liquid outer core.

Crust   The outermost layer of the Earth. The solid surface of the planet.

Daughter element   The element that is formed when the parent element undergoes radioactive decay.

Decay rate The speed at which a radioactive element changes from parent element to daughter element.

Divergent boundary The area where two tectonic plates move away from each other.

Earthquake The shaking of Earth's surface caused by the movement of the crust along a fault zone.

Epicenter The point on Earth's surface directly above the place where an earthquake occurs.

Fault A crack in the crust of the Earth along which usually some movement occurs.

Focus The point inside the Earth where an earthquake occurs.

Fossil The remains of past life preserved in solid rock.

Gondwana A former supercontinent made up of South America, Africa, Antarctica, Australia, and India.

Granite A type of igneous rock that is rich in quartz and is found mostly on the continents.

Half-life The time it takes one-half of a radioactive parent element to turn into a daughter element.

Hypothesis An explanation for a set of observations that has not been tested yet.

Igneous rock A rock that crystallizes from liquid magma.

Inner core The central part of the Earth thought to be made up of solid iron and nickel.

Isostasy The tendency for low-density rock material to rest higher on Earth's surface than high-density rock.

Lava Hot liquid rock that comes out of a volcano.

Lithosphere The upper 60 miles (100 km) of Earth's surface containing both the crust and upper mantle.

Magma Hot liquid rock located inside the Earth.

Magnetic anomaly An area on the surface of the Earth where the planet's magnetic field is either higher or lower than normal.

Magnetic reversal   A point in time when Earth's magnetic field flips, making the north magnetic pole into the south magnetic pole.

Mantle   The layer of the Earth below the crust but above the core.

Meteorology   The study of weather and climate.

Mid-ocean ridge   A divergent boundary where new crust forms. The mid-ocean ridge runs through the North Atlantic Ocean and circles the globe, making it the longest mountain chain on the planet.

Moho (Mohorovicic Discontinuity)   The layer between the crust and the mantle; it was discovered by and named for Andrija Mohorovicic.

North magnetic pole   The point on Earth where the lines of the magnetic field come together. Compasses point to the north magnetic pole.

Outer core   The liquid part of the core that surrounds the solid inner core and lies below the mantle.

P-wave   Longitudinal wave generated by an earthquake that travels at high speed and is usually the first to arrive at a seismograph.

Pangaea   A supercontinent first described by Alfred Wegener back in 1915 demonstrating how all the continents were once joined together in the distant past.

Parent element   A radioactive element that naturally changes or decays into another element called the daughter element.

Polar wandering   The apparent motion of the north magnetic pole around our planet over time.

Radiation   The energy released by the radioactive decay of different elements.

Radioactive decay   The process where one element turns into another while releasing radiation.

Radioactivity   The natural breakdown of an atom into a different type of atom.

Relative age date   The age of a rock or event when compared to another rock. The exact age in years is not known.

Remnant magnetism   Phenomenon where magnetite crystals in Earth's magma harden to form magnetic crystals that act as little microscopic compass needles pointing to Earth's north magnetic pole.

S-wave   Secondary or shear wave that is generated by an earthquake and is usually the second type to arrive at a seismograph.

Sediment   Small pieces of broken rock.

Sedimentary rock   A rock, like a sandstone, that is made from pieces of other rock.

Seismic wave   The type of wave produced by an earthquake.

Seismologist   A scientist who studies how earthquakes behave.

Seismology   The branch of Earth science that studies earthquakes and their causes.

Sial   The upper layer of crust on the continents, made up of rocks made from the chemical elements aluminum and silica.

Sima   The lower layer of crust on the continents and the only layer of crust under oceans. Composed of rocks rich in the chemical elements silicon and magnesium.

Sonar   A device that uses reflected sound waves to locate the seafloor or an object underwater.

Subduction   The process where a piece of oceanic plate is recycled by plunging back down into the mantle.

Subduction zone   A trench in the ocean where subduction takes place.

Submarine trench   A large rip in the crust of the Earth.

Tectonic plate   A large piece of the outer surface of Earth that moves around the planet.

Transform fault   A fault found mostly in oceans that cuts across other submarine features like the mid-ocean ridge and trenches.

Uniformitarianism The principle that says big changes are sometimes caused by small changes that take place over a long period of time.

Volcano A surface feature of Earth through which lava and ash come up from below.

Bibliography

Bryson, Bill. *A Short History of Nearly Everything.* New York: Broadway Books, 2003.

Cernak, Linda. *Everything You Need to Teach Volcanoes.* Bethesda, Md.: Teachers A-Z Resource Books Discovery Communications, 1999.

Coch, Nicholas and Allan Ludman. *Physical Geology.* New York: Macmillan, 1991.

Gribbin, John. *The Scientists.* New York: Random House, 2002.

Hewitt, Paul. *Conceptual Physics.* 8th ed. New York: Addison-Wesley, 1998.

Lamb, Simon and David Sington. *Earth Story: The Forces That Have Shaped Our Planet.* Princeton, N.J.: Princeton University Press, 1998.

Robinson, Andrew. *Earthshock.* London: Thames and Hudson, 1993.

Seyfert, Carl and Leslie Sirkin. *Earth History and Plate Tectonics.* 2nd ed. New York: Harper & Row, 1979.

Spaulding, Nancy and Samuel Namowitz. *Earth Science.* Evanston, Ill.: D.C. Heath, 1999

Tomecek, Stephen M. *What a Great Idea! Inventions That Changed the World.* New York: Scholastic, 2003.

Tomecek, Steve. *Earthquakes.* Bethesda, Md.: Teachers A-Z Resource Guide Discovery Communications, 2000.

Further Resources

Books

Lohr, James, ed. *Smithsonian Earth.* New York: DK Publishing, 2003.

Mathez, Edmond, ed. *Earth Inside and Out.* New York: New Press, 2001.

Meissner, Rolf. *The Little Book of Planet Earth.* New York: Copernicus Books, 2002.

Piel, Gerard. *The Age of Science, What Scientists Learned in the 20th Century.* New York: Basic Books, 2001.

Ritchie, David and Alexander Gates. *Encyclopedia of Earthquakes and Volcanoes.* New York: Checkmark Books, 2001.

Thompson, Luke. *Earthquakes.* New York: Children's Press, 2000.

Web Sites

Beyond Discovery: The Path from Research to Human Benefit—When the Earth Moves
http://www.beyonddiscovery.org/content/view.article.asp?a=229
> *An overview of the development of plate tectonic theory and its impacts on our lives.*

A Science Odyssey: People and Discoveries
http://www.pbs.org/wgbh/aso/databank/index.html
> *A databank of 120 great scientific discoveries made in the twentieth century.*

United States Geological Survey (USGS): Men and Women of Seismology
http://earthquake.usgs.gov/learning/topics/people.php
> *A collection of biographies about famous seismologists. Site also includes links to current information about earthquakes.*

USGS: This Dynamic Earth
The Story of Plate Tectonics
http://pubs.usgs.gov/gip/dynamic/dynamic.html

> *An informative introduction to the history and impact of plate tectonic theory.*

Yale University Department of Geology and Geophysics
The Origins and Early History of Earth Sciences at Yale
http://www.geology.yale.edu/graduate/history.html

> *A collection of biographies of some of the famous men and women Earth scientists who either worked at or graduated from Yale University.*

Picture Credits

Index

A

absolute time, 41, 45
acoustic projectors, 50
Aden, Gulf of, 84
age of Earth
    catastrophism and,
       11–12
    magnetic anomalies
       and, 62
    radioactiv dating and,
       37, 38–42, 82–83
Alps, 32, 36
Appalachian Mountains,
   32
Argand, Emile, 36
asthenosphere, 78
Atlantic Ocean
    formation of, 24–25
    mapping of, 19
    mountain chain in, 54
    Wegener and, 32, 33
atomic clock, 37
atoms, radioactivity and,
   38, 39
Australia, 86

B

basalts, 29, 74
Becquerel, Henri, 37–38
beta decay, 39
Birch, Albert Francis,
   67
Boltwood, Bertram,
   41–42, 45
Bowie Medal, 72
Buckland, William, 15
Bullard, Edward, 83–84

C

catastrophism
    Atlantic Ocean and,
       24–25
    disproving of, 17
    modern-day, 16
    overview of, 11–12
centrifugal force, 33–34
climate, 32
climate change and,
   85–86
consensus, 9
continental crust, 83–84
continental drift. See
   also Wegener, Alfred
    contracting Earth
       theory and, 20
    contraction theory
       and, 23
    convection and, 45–48
    criticism of, 33–34
    early ideas on, 23–25
    evidence for, 29–33
    overview of, 18–20
    plate tectonics vs., 79
    seafloor spreading
       and, 56
continental shelves,
   83–84
contracting Earth
   theory, 20, 23, 46–47
convection, overview
   of, 47
convection currents,
   45–48, 84–87
convergent boundaries,
   80, 84

conveyor belt, oceanic,
   55–57, 60–63
Copernicus, Nicolaus, 7
cores, 57, 62, 67–68, 72
crust, defined, 68
Curie, Marie and Pierre,
   38
Cuvier, Georges, 12

D

Dana, James, 21, 25
Darwin, Charles, 7, 17
dating techniques,
   41–45
daughter elements, 43
decay rate, 43
decay series, 39
deep focus earthquakes,
   77–78
density
    convection currents
       and, 84
    core of Earth and, 67
    granite, basalt and, 29
    recycling and, 83
divergent boundaries,
   80, 84
Du Toit, Alexander, 36
dynamo effect, 57

E

Earth
    age of, 11–12, 37,
       38–42, 62, 82–83
    layers of, 67–68
    paleomagnetic field of,
       57–58

earthquakes
  mapping of, 74–77
  Mohorovicic and, 73
  overview of, 64–66
  plate boundaries and,
    80
  Richter Scale and,
    68–69
  subduction zones and,
    77–78
Elementary Seismology
  (Richter), 69
Elements of Geology
  (Lyell), 17
*Entstehung der
  Kontinente und Ozeane,
  Die* (Wegener), 27–29
epicenters, 66
evolution, 7, 17, 86

F

faults, 54–55
focus, 66, 77–78
forces, continental drift
  and, 33–34, 36, 84–87
fossils, 10, 12, 55
Fuji, Mount, 76

G

Galapagos Islands, 49
geologic time scale, 41
geology, overview of,
  8–10
glaciers, 29
Gondwana, 23, 86
granites, 29
Greenland, 26, 29,
  32–35
Gulf of Aden, 84
Gutenberg, Beno, 66–67,
  68–69
Guyot, Arnold, 52

H

half-lives, 42, 43
Hawaii, 49
heat, radioactive decay
  and, 47

Heezen, Bruce C.,
  52–54, 60
Hess, Harry Hammond,
  52, 55–57, 77
Highlands (Scotland),
  32
Himalaya Mountains,
  32, 83
History of Ocean Basins
  (Hess), 56
Holmes, Arthur, 45–48,
  84
hot spots, 84
Hutton, James, 12–14
hydrophones, 51
hypotheses, 9

I

ice ages, 86
Iceland, 49, 54
igneous rocks, 9, 45
*Illustrations of the
  Huttonian Theory of
  the Earth* (Playfair),
  13, 15
Indian Ocean, 32
interdisciplinary
  approach, 28
islands, 49
isostasy, 29

J

Jeffreys, Harold, 66–67
Joly, John, 41

K

Kelvin (Lord), 41
Krakatau, 76

L

land bridges, 29
lava, 10, 58
Lehmann, Inge, 71–72
Lehmann Discontinuity,
  72
Lehmann Medal, 72
lithosphere, 80

low-velocity zone, 78
Lyell, Charles, 13,
  14–17
Lyell, Mary, 17

M

magma, 9, 21, 77
magnetic anomalies, 60
magnetic fields, 57–58
magnetic poles, 58
magnetic reversals,
  60–62
malaria, 45
mantle, 68, 78, 86
maps
  Atlantic Ocean and,
    19
  polar wandering and,
    59
  Snider-Pelligrini and,
    24–25
  sonar and, 51
  Tharp and, 53–54
  Wegener and, 29,
    31–32
Mason, Ronald, 60
Matthews, Drummond,
  60–62
McKenzie, Dan, 79–80
Mercalli, Guiseppe,
  68–69
Mercalli scale, 68–69
metamorphic rocks, 45
meteorology
  Mohorovicic and, 73
  Wegener and, 25–26,
    32, 34
mid-ocean ridges, 54,
  62, 82
Mohorovicic, Andrija,
  68–69, 73
Mohorovicic
  Discontinuity, 73
monotremes, 86
mountains. *See also
  Specific mountains*
  continental drift and,
    32, 36, 46–47

formation of, 25
oceans and, 54
Mozambique, 45

N

naturalists, 12
natural selection, 7
neutral boundaries, 80
neutrons, 39
Noah, 12
Norlund, N.E., 71–72
nuclei, 39

O

oceans
   mapping of, 52–54
   seafloor spreading
      and, 55–57
   views of, 49–51
*Origin of the Species
   by Means of Natural
   Selection, On the*
   (Darwin), 7
*Origins of Continents
   and Oceans, The*
   (Wegener), 27–29
Ortelius, Abraham, 19

P

Pacific Ocean, 52, 80
Paget, Francois, 19
paleomagnetic fields,
   57–58, 60–62
Pangaea
   Bullard fit and, 83–84
   climate and, 85–86
   convection currents
      and, 48
   Wegener and, 32
parent elements, 43
Parker, Robert, 79–80
Pinatubo, Mount, 76
plates, defined, 8, 82
Playfair, John, 13, 15
polar wandering,
   58–60
poles, 57, 58–60
"P' paper" (Lehmann),
   72

primary waves. *See*
   P-waves
Principles of Geology
   (Lyell), 15, 17
*Principles of Physical
   Geology* (Holmes), 45
protons, 39
P-waves, 65–66, 71–72,
   78

R

radioactive decay
   atomic time and, 42
   convection and, 47
   crust age and, 82–83
   overview of, 39
radioactivity
   age dating using,
      43–45
   atomic time and,
      41–42
   causes of, 39
   discovery of, 36–37
Raff, Arthur, 60
Rainier, Mount, 76
recycling, 83
Red Sea, 84
refraction, 68–69
relative age dates, 38–41
religion, 11–12, 24–25
remnant magnetism, 58
Richter, Charles, 66–67,
   68–69
Richter Scale, 68–69
rifts, 54, 84
rift zones, 84
Ring of Fire, 76
Runcorn, Stanley, 58–60
Rutherford, Ernest, 38, 42

S

Sahara Desert, 32
San Andreas Fault, 80
scientific method, 9
scientific revolutions, 7
seafloor spreading
   magnetic reversals
      and, 60–63
   overview of, 55–57

questions about, 84
   transform faults and,
      82
secondary waves. *See*
   S-waves
sedimentary rocks, 10,
   13–14, 45
seismic waves, 65–66,
   73
seismographs, 65–66
seismology, 65–69,
   71–72
shear waves. *See* S-waves
sial layer, 72–74
sima layer, 74
Snider-Pelligrini,
   Antonio, 23–25
sonar, 50–52
soundings, 49
Spitsbergen, 32
St. Helens, Mount, 76
subduction zones, 56,
   77–78, 80
submarines, 51
submarine trenches,
   54, 82
Suess, Eduard, 21, 23, 25
supercontinents, 23
S-waves, 66, 78

T

Tambora, Mount, 76
Taylor, Frank Bursley,
   25
tectonic plates, defined,
   80
telegraph cables, 49
Tharp, Marie, 52–54, 60
theories, 9
Theory of the Earth
   (Hutton), 14
Thesaurus Geographicus
   (Ortelius), 19
Thomson, William, 41
tides, 33–34
tillites, 32
time, 38–41, 41–42, 45
transform faults, 80, 82
trenches, 54, 82

U

U-boats, 51
uniformitarianism,
  12–14, 16, 20–21
uranium, 38, 39, 42, 45
Ussher, James, 11

V

Vema, 52–54
Vine, Frederick, 60–63
volcanoes, 9–10, 54,
  75–77

W

wandering poles, 58–60
Wegener, Alfred
  criticism of, 33–34
  death of, 34–35
  interdisciplinary
    approach of, 28
  work of, 17, 25–33
William Bowie Medal,
  72
Wilson, J. Tuzo, 62–63,
  82

X

X-rays, 38

About the Author

Steve Tomecek is a geologist and author of more than 30 non-fiction books for both children and teachers. He works as a consultant and writer for the National Geographic Society and Scholastic, Inc. Tomecek was the writer and host of the Emmy Award–winning television series *Dr. Dad's Phantastic Physical Phenomena.*